READY STEADY COOK ®

the ten-minute cookbook

Compiled and edited by Orla Broderick

Introduction by Ainsley Harriott, with recipes from Antony Worrall Thompson, Brian Turner, Gino D'Acampo, James Martin, James Tanner, Lesley Waters, Nick Nairn, Paul Rankin, Phil Vickery, Ross Burden and Tony Tobin.

BBC
BOOKS

contents

Ainsley Harriott

The one question everyone always asks me is this: do the chefs *really* not know what's in the shopping bag before it is emptied in front of them? I can honestly say they don't, which is why, in my opinion, the show retains so much freshness and energy.

Most of you will be aware of the format. Two contestants come onto the show with around £5–10 worth of food, and with the help of two celebrity chefs they have to come up with a meal in just twenty minutes. Then, to round off the show, it's 'Ainsley's Quickie Bag Challenge'. I tip out a bag of food in front of the two chefs and they have to come up with recipe ideas that can be made in under *ten* minutes. The studio audience votes for the recipes they like the sound of best and the winning chef gets cooking, usually with me and the losing chef joining in the hectic preparation, and a large element of chaos and lots of ad-libbing along the way. To add to the pressure the chef is under, a viewer's question about a cookery problem gets thrown in and the chef has to answer that too.

There's definitely a buzz around the studio before the Quickie Bag Challenge kicks off – the chefs are brimming with nervous energy, and some have a serious

competitive streak. Would you believe they keep a tally of who has had the most wins during a series? And the chefs have to cook the dish in the time. The audience joins in the final countdown and there's no room for cheating. But it's fantastic fun. We're one big happy family. That doesn't mean it's easy on the chefs! To make good television they not only have to cook well but they have to be great performers and masters of the soundbite – it's a lot more tricky than it looks, believe me.

But here we've done all the hard work for you. It never ceases to amaze me the brilliant dishes that the chefs continue to come up with, time after time – and it's those quickie recipes that have inspired this fabulous book. Every one of these recipes can be made at home in under ten minutes, and there are recipes for everything from quick after-work snacks to intimate dinners for two. After all, who wants to spend all their time in the kitchen when they've got a hot date around?

Quality ingredients make all the difference to the finished dish, even more so when you're under time pressure. Fresh, exotic produce from around the world is appearing in our shops in abundance and it is our good fortune that we can experience it. In an ideal world we would shop daily for fresh produce from the best local suppliers but in reality this simply is not possible for most of us, so a well-stocked larder and some planning ahead are key. Convenience foods also play an important part in many of these recipes, providing valuable short-cuts that save you time and effort without loss of flavour.

Remember, too, recipes aren't carved in stone; if you find at the last minute you haven't got an ingredient, or perhaps don't even like it, leave it out or replace it with something you do like. Don't be afraid to improvise – the *Ready Steady Cook* chefs do it all the time. *Ready Steady Cook* is about putting together a delicious dish from whatever ingredients you have to hand. It's also about enjoying yourself in the kitchen. So what are you waiting for? On your marks, get set, go!

THE CHEFS

Antony Worrall Thompson MOGB, FHCIMA

A restaurateur for over twenty years, Antony's flagship restaurant is Notting Grill in Holland Park, which specializes in organic meat, fish and vegetables, and more recently he has opened Kew Grill on Kew Green and three further country gastro pubs, The Lamb at Satwell, The Greyhound at Rotherfield Peppard and The Angel Coaching Inn at Heytesbury. Newest of all is the Barnes Grill, which opened in summer 2006.

He has been awarded the Meilleur Ouvrier de Grande Bretagne (MOGB) – the chefs' Oscar – and is one of only seven chefs in Britain to have merited the lifelong title.

Antony has been a *Ready Steady Cook* regular for many years, he was resident chef for BBC2's *Food and Drink* programme and the presenter of *Saturday Kitchen*, BBC1's weekly live cookery programme. He has been a guest on many TV programmes, including *Panorama* and *Question Time*. Antony emerged as one of the nation's favourite celebrities in the ITV series *I'm A Celebrity Get Me Out of Here* in spring 2003.

He writes for *The Express on Sunday Magazine* and Saturday *Express*, and has written many cookery books – among the latest a children's cookbook called *Real Family Food*, *The GI Diet Made Simple* and, newest of all, *Barbecues & Grilling*. His autobiography is called *Raw*.

Brian Turner CBE

Brian trained at some of the most prestigious hotels and restaurants in Europe, earning himself a prized Michelin star, which he held for ten years, before opening his own restaurant, Turner's, in Walton Street, Knightsbridge. In 2003 Brian Turner Mayfair was launched at the Millennium Hotel London Mayfair, and 2005 saw the opening of Turner's Grill at the Copthorne Hotel Slough-Windsor, with Gatwick, Birmingham and Plymouth the next to open.

As a no-nonsense, straight-talking Yorkshireman, Brian has been a champion of British produce and British cooking over the last twenty-five years. A regular guest on *Ready Steady Cook* since the programme began, he has been a judge on *Masterchef*, appeared on *Food and Drink*, and was the resident chef on Granada's *This Morning* for many years before hosting his own series, *Out to Lunch*, *A Yorkshire Pudding* and *Anything You Can Cook*, for the BBC. In 2002 Her Majesty the Queen honoured Brian with a CBE for his services to tourism and training in the catering industry.

Gino D'Acampo

Many chefs have led colourful lives but few can match Gino's. Born into a humble Neapolitan family, he has worked in France, Spain and Britain, cooked for Pavarotti and now forged a successful career in television. Gino inherited his love of cooking from his grandfather, a head chef in Naples. He entered the Luigi de Medici Catering College at the age of fifteen, from where he was sent each summer to gain experience in kitchens across Europe.

He joined a major Italian food supplier in England, and his skills in blending olive oil led to his first foray into television. He has since made regular appearances on a number of shows, including *This Morning* and *Too Many Cooks* on ITV, *The Terry and Gaby Show* on Five and *Saturday Kitchen* and *Ready Steady Cook* on the BBC. His own series include *Chef V. Britain* for ITV and two series of *An Italian In Mexico* for UKTV Food. Gino lives in London with his wife Jessica and sons Luciano and Rocco.

James Martin

James Martin has made a great impact since he began to appear on *Ready Steady Cook* in November 1996 and has rarely been off screen since. In 2005 he gained an additional army of fans with his new-found prowess on the dance floor in *Strictly Come Dancing* (BBC1), where he reached the semi-finals.

He was Student of the Year for three years running at Scarborough Technical College, worked at Chewton Glen, and in 1994 at the tender age of twenty-two he opened the Hotel and Bistro du Vin in Winchester as Head Chef. He has two of his own restaurants on the cruise ships *Ocean Village* and *Ocean Village 2*.

He is the resident chef on *Castle in the Country* for BBC2, was the resident chef on BBC's *Housecall*, has had several of his own series for Carlton and UKTV Food, and made countless guest appearances on many TV shows, including being a regular contributor to *Saturday Kitchen*. Recent TV appearances include *Richard & Judy*, *Petrolheads* and the *Stately Suppers* series. His most recent books are *Great British Dinners* and *Easy British Food*. He is currently making his own gardening and cooking series for UKTV Food. He is a hugely popular demonstrator at food and drink festivals across the UK and is chairman of the judges of the Nestlé Toque d'Or student chef competition 2006.

James Tanner

The third of four brothers, James was brought up in Kent and taught to cook by his mother. He studied hotel management and worked his way up through the ranks in the kitchens of several well-known restaurants. His talent was spotted by the Roux Brothers, who invited him to work as chef de partie at the Lake Placid Lodge in upstate New York. He was quickly promoted to junior sous-chef, and then transferred to the prestigious Point restaurant.

Back in England James worked for the respected chef Martin Blunos at the two-Michelin-starred restaurant Lettonie in Bath, later becoming head chef at Right on the Green in Kent. In 1999, aged twenty-three, James opened Tanners Restaurant in Plymouth with his brother Chris. In 2006 they opened a bistro, The Barbican Kitchen, in the original Plymouth Gin distillery.

Following James's first television appearance in 2001, Ainsley Harriott recommended him to the *Ready Steady Cook* team and he has since become a regular guest. James also appears on *Saturday Kitchen* and *This Morning*, and he and Chris have also filmed their own series, *The Tanner Brothers*. The brothers' first book is *Chocolate Lovers' Cookbook*.

Lesley Waters

A former chef and cookery demonstrator, Lesley eventually became head teacher at Leith's School of Food & Wine, where she perfected her cookery demonstration and food photography skills, and often represented British food at international cookery displays. Lesley has worked in television since 1989 and her work has included writing and presenting numerous series for the BBC, Superchannel, Carlton Food Network, UKTV Food and Anglia. Her lively personality makes her a popular television cook and a regular member of the team on BBC 1's *Ready Steady Cook* and a frequent guest on both *Great Food Live* (UKTV Food), BBC 1's *Saturday Kitchen* and ITV's *This Morning*.

Lesley is a regular contributor to *BBC Good Food Magazine* and *Big Cook Little Cook*. She has written nearly twenty books, and her latest titles include *New To Cooking* and *Healthy Food*. She has also produced a series of paperback cookbooks with food retailer Julian Graves.

Most recently she has opened her own cookery school, where she hosts themed cooking days at her country home in Dorset.

Nick Nairn

A self-taught chef, Nick started his career in the merchant navy, but his passion for cooking soon led him to open his first restaurant, Braeval, in 1986. By 1991 he was Scotland's youngest Michelin-starred chef, and in 1997 he opened Nairns restaurant to international acclaim.

Nick is a popular guest on *Ready Steady Cook* and has presented several television series, including *Wild Harvest*, *Island Harvest* and *Nick Nairn and the Dinner Ladies*, which won a Glenfiddich award in 2004.

Nick is based at his state-of-the-art Cook School near Stirling and is an active champion of fresh local produce. He has written nine cookery books, including *Nick Nairn's Top 100 Salmon Recipes* and *New Scottish Cookery*.

Paul Rankin

A regular on *Ready Steady Cook*, Paul has a successful restaurant and café business in his native Northern Ireland, which he runs with his wife and fellow chef, Jeanne. Paul and Jeanne worked together at Le Gavroche, the Roux brothers' restaurant in London, and on their return to Belfast they set up their first restaurant, Roscoff, which won Northern Ireland's first Michelin star. In addition to Roscoff, Paul and Jeanne also operate Cayenne, Rain City Grill and a plethora of Paul Rankin Cafés throughout Ireland, all supplied by their own bakery.

Paul has appeared with Jeanne in many television programmes, including *The Rankin Challenge*, *Masterchef* and three series of *Gourmet Ireland*. They have published several successful books, including *New Irish Cookery* and two volumes of *Gourmet Ireland*. In addition to *Ready Steady Cook,* Paul is also a frequent guest on BBC1's *Saturday Kitchen*.

Paul recently worked as consultant to a care home in Belfast, devising appetizing menus tailor-made for the nutritional needs of the elderly, which led to invitations to address conferences and a *Tonight with Trevor McDonald* programme on the issue.

Phil Vickery

Phil was born in Folkestone, Kent. Following his training in the Lake District, he went on to work at Gravetye Manor in West Sussex, followed by a short stint at Ian McAndrew's Restaurant 74 in Canterbury, and nine years at the Castle Hotel in Taunton, Somerset. During his time there, the restaurant was named *Times* Restaurant of the Year and was awarded Michelin and Egon Ronay stars four years in a row.

Phil has appeared on the BBC's *Ready Steady Cook* and *Masterchef*, ITV's *This Morning*, and *Phil Vickery's Pudding Club*, his own television series for Anglia. Phil's books include *Just Food* and *The Proof of the Pudding*, and he also writes a regular column for a Sunday newspaper and features for several magazines. He is married to TV presenter Fern Britton.

Ross Burden

Model-turned-presenter Ross Burden has featured on television shows in Britain and around the world since reaching the final of the BBC's *Masterchef* competition in 1993. Although he is perhaps best known for his culinary skills on *Ready Steady Cook*, Ross is also a trained naturalist and keen traveller; a degree in zoology and an upbringing on the New Zealand coast have equipped him to explore the natural world for *National Geographic* and *Network of the World*. He has also filmed a healthy-eating video with Joan Collins and has made five series for Taste Television. Ross regularly appears at major food festivals and teaches at several internationally renowned cookery schools, including Villa Valentina and Nairn's Cook School. He is the author of *Food for All Seasons*.

Tony Tobin

Tony started cooking professionally at the age of fourteen when he worked in the kitchens of a pub-restaurant in Warwickshire. After two years at Stratford-upon-Avon Catering College, he worked in a succession of prestigious restaurants, including Chez Nico and Simply Nico (under Nico Ladenis) and the restaurant of the Capital Hotel (under Brian Turner). He is now the chef-proprietor of the Dining Room in Reigate, Surrey.

Tony has made guest appearances on many television programmes, including *Food and Drink* and *This Morning*, and has appeared regularly on *Saturday Kitchen*, *Ready Steady Cook* and *Can't Cook, Won't Cook*. He also presented *Spice World* and *The Green Gourmet* for Carlton Food Network. Tony's recipes have featured in several books, including *Hot Chefs*, *Ready Steady Cook: The Top 100 Recipes* and *The Twelve Chefs of Christmas*.

starters

Antony Worrall Thompson
SMOKED TROUT AND
WATERCRESS PÂTÉ

Mackerel smokes very well; the oiliness of the fish prevents it from drying out. Avoid the ones dyed with tartrazine – easy to spot as the fish will have a golden-yellow tinge to it.

Serves 2

1 small French baguette
2 tbsp extra-virgin olive oil
25 g (1 oz) walnut halves
75 g (3 oz) smoked mackerel fillet
25 g (1 oz) watercress, well picked over, tough stalks removed, plus extra to garnish
1 tbsp Dijon mustard
25 g (1 oz) butter, softened
juice ½ lemon
about 1 tbsp crème fraiche
salt and freshly ground black pepper

Preheat the oven to 180°C/350°F/Gas 4. Cut the baguette into 0.5 cm (¼ in) slices, dribble with half of the olive oil and arrange on a baking sheet. Place in the oven for about 8 minutes or until crisp and golden.

Place the walnuts in a dry frying pan and lightly toast, tossing occasionally to ensure that they cook evenly. Tip out onto a flat plate and leave to cool completely, then roughly chop.

Strip the mackerel flesh from the skin, discarding the skin, and place the flesh in a food processor. Add the watercress, mustard, butter, lemon juice and remaining olive oil. Blend until smooth and then season to taste.

Divide half of the mackerel mixture between two 6 cm (2½ in) metal cooking rings that have been set on plates and scatter the walnuts on top. Cover with the remaining mackerel mixture and then carefully spread over a layer of crème fraiche to come up to the top of each cooking ring. Garnish with the watercress and serve at once with the toasts piled high to the side.

‘Watercresscendo’

starters

13

James Martin
TOMATO TART WITH BASIL OIL

A very simple tart, eaten with a fresh-tasting basil oil. Try to use mozzarella made from buffalo milk. It's creamier and much richer than the cow's milk version, which can be rubbery and bland. ▸

Serves 2

175 g (6 oz) sheet ready-rolled puff
   pastry, thawed if frozen
1 egg yolk, lightly beaten
6 mini mozzarella balls, sliced
   (buffalo if possible)
handful small fresh basil leaves
8 small cherry tomatoes, halved
a little olive oil

FOR THE BASIL OIL
juice 1 lemon
4 tbsp extra-virgin olive oil
1 garlic clove, roughly chopped
good handful fresh basil leaves
salt and freshly ground black pepper

Preheat the oven to 220°C/425°F/Gas 7. Cut the pastry into two 10 cm (4 in) circles and place on a large baking sheet. Brush with the egg yolk and prick all over with a fork.

Scatter the mozzarella balls, basil leaves and cherry tomatoes on top. Season to taste and add a drizzle of olive oil to the basil leaves to prevent them from burning. Bake for 8–9 minutes until the pastry is crisp and golden.

To make the basil oil, place the lemon juice, olive oil, garlic and basil in a mini food processor and blend until smooth. Season to taste.

When the tarts are cooked, transfer to warmed plates and drizzle over the basil oil to serve.

James Tanner
GRIDDLED TOMATOES WITH ARTICHOKES AND PARMESAN CRISPS

This simple starter is a masterpiece – everyone will be blown away by the flavours, as long as you use good quality ingredients.

Serves 2

100 g (4 oz) piece Parmesan
3 small ripe plum tomatoes
good pinch caster sugar
pinch chilli powder
olive oil, for cooking
100 g (4 oz) artichoke hearts preserved
   in olive oil, drained and halved
2 tbsp chopped fresh flat-leaf parsley
salt and freshly ground black pepper

Preheat the oven to 220°C/425°F/Gas 7 and heat a griddle pan until very hot. Finely grate the Parmesan and arrange six small piles on a non-stick baking sheet, well spaced apart. Bake for 5–6 minutes until crisp and golden. Remove from the oven and leave to cool.

Meanwhile, cut the plum tomatoes in half and sprinkle over the sugar and chilli powder. Drizzle the heated griddle pan with a little oil and add the tomatoes, cut side down. Cook for 2–3 minutes until nicely marked, then turn over and cook for another 1–2 minutes until well heated through.

Arrange the griddled tomatoes on plates with the artichoke hearts and season to taste. Scatter over the parsley and then pile up the Parmesan crisps to the side to serve.

Phil Vickery

ROASTED PEARS WRAPPED IN BLACK FOREST HAM WITH ROCKET SALAD

This salad not only looks and tastes fabulous, it is also incredibly easy to make.

Serves 2

1 ripe firm pear
100 g (4 oz) thin slices Black Forest ham
25 g (1 oz) butter
4 tbsp brandy
25 g (1 oz) walnut halves, chopped
50 g (2 oz) wild rocket
2 tbsp snipped fresh chives
2 tbsp chopped fresh flat-leaf parsley
2 tbsp chopped fresh dill
175 g (6 oz) Cashel blue cheese
salt and freshly ground black pepper

Heat a large frying pan. Peel the pear and cut into quarters, then remove the core and thinly slice. Cut the Black Forest ham into strips and quickly wrap one round each slice of pear.

Add the butter to the heated frying pan and once it is foaming, add the wrapped pear slices. Cook for 2–3 minutes until crisp, turning once. Pour in the brandy and allow to flambé. Scatter in the walnuts and continue to toss until all the flames have died down and the liquid has evaporated.

Arrange the rocket on plates and scatter the chives, parsley and dill on top. Season to taste, then divide the wrapped pear slices and walnuts between them. Break up the Cashel blue into small pieces, discarding the rind, and scatter on top to serve.

Antony Worrall Thompson

GRIDDLED RICOTTA-STUFFED FIGS WRAPPED IN PARMA HAM WITH ROCKET

The combination of warm figs and salty, crisp Parma ham is sublime and needs nothing more than the dressed rocket leaves to serve.

Serves 2

2 tbsp ricotta cheese
1 tbsp shredded fresh basil
6 ripe figs
6 thin slices Parma ham
50 g (2 oz) wild rocket
1 tsp balsamic vinegar
2 tbsp extra-virgin olive oil
salt and freshly ground black pepper

Heat a griddle pan until very hot. Place the ricotta in a bowl with the basil and season to taste. Cut a cross into the top of each fig and then, using a teaspoon, stuff with the ricotta mixture.

Wrap each stuffed fig in a slice of Parma ham and add to the heated griddle pan. Cook for 4–5 minutes until the Parma ham is crispy and the figs are heated through, turning occasionally.

Place the rocket in a bowl and add the balsamic vinegar and olive oil. Season generously and then toss until the leaves are evenly coated. Divide between plates and arrange the griddled figs on top to serve.

Brian Turner
ASPARAGUS WRAPPED IN PANCETTA

We figured it out and it came out pancetta than we thought

This is best during asparagus season, which runs for approximately eight weeks in May and June. This is when asparagus has a full, sweet flavour and fine, tender texture.

Serves 2

14 asparagus spears
14 thin slices pancetta (Italian streaky bacon)
1 tbsp olive oil

FOR THE BLUSHED CHIVE DIP
100 g (4 oz) soft cream cheese
2 tbsp Greek yoghurt
6 sun-blushed tomatoes
small bunch fresh chives, snipped
salt and freshly ground black pepper

Heat a griddle pan until very hot. Trim the asparagus spears and then blanch in a pan of boiling water for 2–3 minutes until just tender when pierced with the tip of a sharp knife. Drain and quickly refresh under cold running water, then pat dry on kitchen paper.

Wrap each of the asparagus spears in a slice of pancetta and arrange on a plate. Drizzle with the olive oil and season to taste. Add the wrapped asparagus spears to the heated griddle pan and cook for 3–4 minutes until crisp and lightly golden, turning regularly.

Meanwhile, place the cream cheese in a mini food processor with the yoghurt, sun-blushed tomatoes, chives and seasoning. Blend until smooth.

Arrange stacks of the asparagus wrapped in pancetta on warmed plates with the blushed dip and serve at once.

Nick Nairn
PARMA WRAP WITH MELON

This is an interesting twist on a classic combination. Charentais melon is my favourite. It is round in shape with roughish pale-green skin and fragrant peachy-orange flesh.

Serves 2

juice ½ lemon
1 tsp balsamic vinegar
1 tbsp light muscovado sugar
1 ripe melon (such as charentais)
1 orange
1 bunch watercress, well picked over
1 bunch fresh basil
3 thin slices Parma ham
extra-virgin olive oil, for drizzling

Place the lemon juice in a bowl with the balsamic vinegar. Whisk in the sugar until dissolved. Cut the melon in half and discard the seeds. Using a melon baller, scoop the melon flesh into balls and add to the bowl with the lemon mixture.

Using a very sharp knife, remove the skin from the orange with all the white pith, then cut into segments and add to the bowl. Gently fold together, and set aside to allow the flavours to develop.

Mix the watercress and basil, then separate six even-sized bunches, trimming down any thick stems. Cut the slices of Parma ham in half lengthways and use to wrap each bunch, ensuring the stems are enclosed and the leaves are showing.

Divide the herby wraps between plates and spoon a mound of the marinated melon balls alongside. Drizzle with olive oil and serve at once.

starters

17

Paul Rankin
SEARED PRAWN COCKTAIL

I made this in the programme with raw tiger prawns, but Dublin Bay prawns, otherwise known as langoustines, could be even better.

Serves 4

2 tbsp mayonnaise

2 tbsp Greek yoghurt

1 tbsp tomato ketchup

½ tsp clear honey, or sugar to taste

dash Worcestershire sauce

few drops Tabasco sauce

pinch medium curry powder

1 lime

225 g (8 oz) raw peeled prawns,
    cleaned (such as Dublin Bay or tiger)

1 tbsp sunflower oil

pinch dried crushed chillies

2 little Gem lettuces, shredded

1 firm ripe avocado

salt and freshly ground black pepper

To make the cocktail dressing, mix together the mayonnaise, Greek yoghurt, tomato ketchup, honey or sugar, Worcestershire sauce, Tabasco and curry powder in a small bowl. Cut the lime in half and add a squeeze to the dressing, then season to taste.

Heat a heavy-based pan. Pat dry the prawns on kitchen paper and tip into a bowl. Add the oil and crushed chillies, and season to taste. Toss until well combined. Add to the pan and sear over a high heat for 1–2 minutes until opaque in colour and just cooked through. Add a good squeeze of lime juice, tossing to coat, and remove from the heat.

Put the shredded lettuce in the bottom of serving dishes. Cut the avocado in half and remove the stone. Peel off the skin and chop or slice the flesh, then scatter over the lettuce. Arrange the seared prawns on top and drizzle over the cocktail dressing. Cut the remaining half of the lime into wedges and use to garnish before serving.

❛ Prawn to be wild ❜

Gino D'Acampo
SMOKED CHICKEN GOUJONS WITH GARLIC AIOLI

If you haven't got time to make your own aioli, simply beat the garlic into a good quality shop-bought mayonnaise along with a couple of tablespoons of good quality olive oil, and I promise no one will know the difference.

Serves 2

sunflower oil, for deep-frying
225 g (8 oz) cooked smoked chicken
  breast, skinned
100 g (4 oz) self-raising flour
1 egg yolk
150 ml (¼ pint) sparkling water
1 baby cos lettuce
squeeze lemon juice
a little extra-virgin olive oil

FOR THE GARLIC AIOLI

1 egg yolk
1 tsp Dijon mustard
1 garlic clove, crushed
½ tsp white wine vinegar
50 ml (2fl oz) sunflower oil
50 ml (2fl oz) extra-virgin olive oil
salt and freshly ground black pepper

Preheat a deep-fat fryer or fill a deep-sided pan one-third full with the sunflower oil and heat to 180°C/350°F. If you don't have a thermometer, the oil should be hot enough so that when a bread cube is added, it browns in 60 seconds.

To make the garlic aioli, beat the egg yolk in a bowl with the mustard, garlic, vinegar, two teaspoons of water and seasoning, until thickened. Mix the oils together in a jug and then begin to add to the egg yolk mixture, drop by drop, whisking constantly. After adding two tablespoons of oil the mixture should be quite thick. Add the remaining oil more quickly, a teaspoon at a time, whisking constantly. Season to taste, then transfer to a plastic squeezy bottle.

To make the smoked goujons, cut the smoked chicken breast into long thin strips. Place the flour, egg yolk and sparkling water in a large bowl and quickly whisk together to form a smooth batter.

Dip the smoked chicken strips into the batter, shaking off any excess and then carefully drop into the heated oil and deep-fry for 2–3 minutes until crisp and golden brown – you may have to do this in batches depending on the size of your pan. Drain on kitchen paper.

Shred the cos lettuce and place in a bowl. Lightly dress the leaves with a squeeze of lemon juice and a little extra-virgin olive oil. Season to taste and place a pile in the middle of each plate. Pile the crispy smoked chicken goujons on top and drizzle around the aioli to serve.

Gino D'Acampo
SMOKED SALMON PÂTÉ WITH TOASTED RYE BAGELS

Chewy toasted bagels are perfect spread thickly with this delicious pâté. You can use any type available, but rye varieties have a particular affinity with the smoked salmon.

Serves 2

2 rye bagels
100 g (4 oz) smoked salmon slices
75 g (3 oz) soft cream cheese
2 tbsp Greek yoghurt
½ tsp creamed horseradish
few drops Tabasco sauce
freshly ground black pepper
2 tiny fresh dill sprigs, to garnish
2 lemon wedges, to serve

Preheat the grill. Cut the rye bagels in half and toast under the grill for 2–3 minutes.

To make the pâté, roughly chop the smoked salmon and place in a mini food processor with the cream cheese, Greek yoghurt, horseradish and Tabasco. Season generously with pepper and whiz until smooth.

Spoon the smoked salmon pâté into individual ramekins and smooth over with a palette knife. Garnish with a dill sprig and set on plates. Arrange the rye bagels and lemon wedges alongside to serve.

Nick Nairn
NATURAL OYSTERS WITH CHILLI SHALLOT VINEGAR

Instead of getting your fishmonger to open the oysters, have a go yourself. An oyster knife is a good investment – make sure you buy one with a guard, and use a tea towel to protect your hand.

Serves 2

12 oysters (native, if possible)

FOR THE CHILLI SHALLOT VINEGAR
100 ml (3½ fl oz) red wine vinegar
1 shallot, very finely diced
½ mild red chilli, seeded and very
  finely chopped
1 tbsp snipped fresh chives
freshly ground black pepper

Combine the ingredients for the chilli shallot vinegar in a small bowl and season with pepper to taste. Set aside to allow the flavours to develop.

Scrub the oyster shells then place one, wrapped in a clean tea towel, on a firm surface with the flattest shell uppermost and the hinge pointing towards you. Gripping the oyster firmly, insert an oyster knife into the gap in the hinge and twist to snap the shells apart.

Slide the blade along the inside of the upper shell to sever the muscle that holds it together. Lift the lid off the top shell, being careful not to spill any juices. Carefully clean away any broken shell and finally run the knife under the oyster to loosen it. Repeat until all the oysters are opened and then arrange on plates.

Spoon a little of the chilli shallot vinegar onto each oyster and serve at once.

starters

21

Antony Worrall Thompson
SCRAMBLED EGGS IN SHELLS WITH CAVIAR AND SMOKED SALMON

Serve this with toast soldiers spread with butter. Long thin slices of toasted flavoured breads also make a nice change: try herby focaccia, black olive or sun-dried tomato ciabatta, or cheese and onion loaf. ▶

Serves 2

2 large eggs
knob unsalted butter
1 tbsp soft cream cheese
1 tsp Dijon mustard
1 tsp caviar
salt and freshly ground black pepper
thin strips smoked salmon and snipped
    fresh chives, to garnish

Carefully crack the top off each egg and drain into a bowl, reserving the shell. Season the eggs and lightly beat together with a fork.

Melt the butter in a heavy-based pan over a low heat. Swirl the butter around the sides of the pan so that it coats the sides. Add the beaten eggs and cook over a medium heat for 2 minutes, or until the eggs are half set. Take the pan off the heat, add the cream cheese and mustard and keep stirring, returning to the heat if necessary, until the eggs are soft and creamy.

Spoon the scrambled eggs back into the shells and set into egg cups, then top each one with half a teaspoon of the caviar. Garnish with a swirl of smoked salmon and a tiny sprinkling of chives.

Ross Burden
AUBERGINE FRITTERS WITH TOMATO RELISH

Leftover tomato relish can be stored in a dish covered with cling film for up to 3–4 days in the fridge. It would liven up any cheese sandwich no end.

Serves 2

sunflower oil, for deep-frying
4 tbsp fresh white breadcrumbs
1 tsp chopped fresh sage
75 g (3 oz) feta cheese, crumbled
4 tbsp seasoned flour
2 eggs, beaten
1 small aubergine, cut into
    1 cm (½ in) slices

FOR THE TOMATO RELISH
1 tbsp olive oil
2 spring onions, finely chopped
1 garlic clove, crushed
2 ripe tomatoes, peeled, quartered
    and seeded
2 tbsp dry white wine
salt and freshly ground black pepper

Heat about 5 cm (2 in) of the sunflower oil in a wok or large deep-sided pan. To make the tomato relish, place the oil in a small frying pan. Add the spring onions and garlic and sauté for 1–2 minutes until softened. Stir in the tomatoes, then add the wine. Season to taste and simmer for 5 minutes until slightly reduced.

Meanwhile, mix together the breadcrumbs, sage and feta in a shallow dish, then place the seasoned flour on a flat plate and the eggs into a separate shallow dish. Dip the aubergine slices into the seasoned flour, then coat in the egg. Toss in the breadcrumb mixture until completely covered, shaking off any excess. Repeat until all the slices are coated.

Deep-fry the aubergine in batches for 2–3 minutes until completely tender and golden brown. Drain well on kitchen paper and keep warm.

Blitz the relish with a hand blender until almost smooth, then transfer to individual dishes set on warmed plates. Pile up the aubergine fritters alongside and serve at once.

Tony Tobin
SWEET AND SOUR PEPPERS WITH GRILLED GOAT'S CHEESE

The flavour of the goat's cheese determines the success of the dish, so choose carefully. The sweet and sour peppers are delicious hot or cold and will last up to a week in the fridge. ◄

Serves 2

2 tbsp olive oil
1 small red onion, thinly sliced
1 red pepper, seeded and cut into batons
50 g (2 oz) uncooked chorizo sausage, skinned and diced
2 x 100g (4 oz) individual soft-rinded goat's cheese
4 tbsp seasoned flour
1 tbsp caster sugar
1 tbsp balsamic vinegar
1 tbsp extra-virgin olive oil
2 tbsp chopped fresh flat-leaf parsley
salt and freshly ground black pepper

Heat a tablespoon of the olive oil in a pan. Add the onion, pepper and chorizo and sauté for 3–4 minutes until tender but without colouring. Season to taste.

Meanwhile, heat a frying pan with the remaining tablespoon of olive oil. Cut each goat's cheese in half horizontally and coat in the flour, shaking off any excess. Add to the heated pan and cook for 2–3 minutes on each side until heated through and lightly golden.

Sprinkle the sugar into the pepper mixture, add the balsamic vinegar, then allow to reduce for another 2–3 minutes.

Remove the sweet and sour peppers from the heat, divide between plates and drizzle over the extra-virgin olive oil. When the goat's cheese is ready, arrange alongside or on top, scatter over the parsley and serve.

Tony Tobin
HOT CHEESE IN A BOX WITH GRIDDLED CIABATTA

This is a great way to use up cheese that won't ripen properly. To help cut through the richness I'd serve this with a bitter leaf salad with a wholegrain mustard dressing.

Serves 2

1 small Camembert (in a wooden box)
olive oil, for drizzling
1 garlic clove, finely chopped
good pinch soft fresh thyme leaves
1 small ciabatta loaf
salt and freshly ground black pepper

Preheat the oven to 220°C/425°F/Gas 7 and heat a griddle pan until searing hot. Remove the wrapper from the Camembert and return the cheese to the wooden box. Season generously and drizzle with olive oil. Sprinkle the garlic and thyme on top and place on a baking sheet. Bake for 6–8 minutes until warmed through and bubbling.

Meanwhile, cut the ciabatta into slices on the diagonal and arrange on the heated griddle pan. Cook for a minute or two on each side until nicely marked, and drizzle with a little olive oil. Depending on the size of your griddle pan, you may have to do this in batches.

Arrange the Camembert in the middle of a large plate and pile the griddled ciabatta around the edges to serve.

❝ I'm very fondue of this cheese ❞

James Martin
PRAWN WONTONS WITH CHILLI JAM

This starter is ideal with a drink (preferably a glass of bubbly). The wontons are simple to make and taste far superior to ready-made versions.

Serves 2

sunflower oil, for deep-frying
6 raw peeled tiger prawns, cleaned
2 spring onions, chopped
1 mild red chilli, seeded and chopped
2.5 cm (1 in) piece fresh root ginger, peeled and chopped
2 garlic cloves, chopped
12 wonton wrappers, thawed if frozen
1 egg, beaten
1 tbsp chopped fresh coriander
½ tsp sesame seeds

FOR THE CHILLI JAM
1 mild red chilli, seeded and chopped
2 spring onions, sliced
1 tsp freshly grated root ginger
1 tbsp sesame seeds
drizzle sesame oil
drizzle dark soy sauce
1 tbsp clear honey
juice 1 lime
salt and freshly ground black pepper

Preheat a deep-fat fryer or fill a deep-sided pan one third full with oil and heat to 190°C/375°F. If you don't have a thermometer, the oil should be hot enough so that when a bread cube is added, it browns in 40 seconds.

Place the prawns in a food processor with the spring onions, chilli, ginger and garlic. Season to taste and blitz for a few seconds until the mixture is well combined.

Place a teaspoon of the prawn mixture in the middle of a wonton wrapper and brush the sides with beaten egg. Fold over to form a triangle and repeat until you have twelve wontons in total. Deep-fry the wontons for 2–3 minutes until cooked through and golden brown.

Meanwhile, make the chilli jam: place the chilli, spring onions, ginger, sesame seeds, sesame oil, soy sauce, honey and lime juice in a mini food processor and blitz for a few seconds until well combined.

Drain the cooked wontons well on kitchen paper and arrange on warmed plates with individual bowls of the chilli jam. Garnish with the coriander and a sprinkling of sesame seeds.

Lesley Waters
CHILLI CRAB CAKES WITH DIPPING SAUCE

A lovely easy starter for an intimate dinner for two. They will whet the appetite and set the tone for the rest of the meal.

Serves 2

50 g (2 oz) fresh white breadcrumbs
175 g (6 oz) white crabmeat, thawed
   if frozen
1 mild red chilli, seeded and finely
   chopped
3 tbsp chopped fresh coriander
1 egg, beaten
good dash dark soy sauce
2 tbsp seasoned flour
sunflower oil, for shallow frying
salt and freshly ground black pepper

FOR THE DIPPING SAUCE
2 tbsp sesame seeds
4 tsp dark soy sauce
2 tsp sesame oil
1 tsp Tabasco sauce
2 tbsp chopped fresh coriander
lime wedges, to serve

Place the breadcrumbs in a food processor with the crabmeat, chilli, coriander, egg, soy sauce and seasoning. Pulse together until just combined.

Divide the mixture into eight and, using slightly dampened hands, shape into patties. Lightly dust in the seasoned flour, shaking off the excess.

Heat 2.5 cm (1 in) of oil in a large frying pan and gently fry the chilli crab cakes for 2–3 minutes on each side until cooked through and golden brown.

Meanwhile, make the dipping sauce. Place the sesame seeds in a bowl with the soy sauce, sesame oil, Tabasco and coriander. Stir to combine and then pour into individual dipping bowls.

Arrange the chilli crab cakes on warmed plates and add a bowl of the dipping sauce to each one. Garnish with lime wedges and serve at once.

' Crab it before it gets chilli '

soups

Phil Vickery
PRAWN BISQUE

It's hard to believe a soup so rich in texture and flavour can be made in less than ten minutes – but it can. You could replace the prawn shells with cracked lobster or crab shells, or use good quality whole shrimps.

Serves 2

knob butter
1 tbsp olive oil
1 shallot, finely chopped
1 celery stick, finely chopped
1 garlic clove, finely chopped
100 g (4 oz) shells from raw tiger prawns
2 sprigs fresh tarragon
2 tbsp brandy
4 tbsp dry white wine
300 ml (½ pint) hot chicken stock
   (from a cube is fine)
100 ml (3½ fl oz) double cream
pinch paprika
squeeze lemon juice
½ tsp snipped fresh chives
salt and freshly ground black pepper

Melt the butter with the oil in a pan and sauté the shallot, celery and garlic for 1–2 minutes until softened but not coloured.

Increase the heat, add the prawn shells to the pan with the tarragon and cook for another minute or two, stirring. Pour in the brandy and allow to reduce right down. Stir in the wine and stock and bring to the boil, then boil fast for 2 minutes to reduce.

Transfer to a blender and blitz to a smooth purée, then strain back into a clean pan through a fine sieve, pressing down with the back of a wooden spoon. Stir in the cream and add the paprika and lemon juice. Season to taste and just heat through.

Ladle the prawn bisque into warmed bowls and add a tiny sprinkling of chives to each one. Serve at once.

'It takes the bisqueit'

Paul Rankin

SMOKY BACON AND TOMATO SOUP WITH GARLIC TOASTS

This soup reminds me of my childhood, when my mum used to push it through a fine strainer with the back of a spoon for a smooth finish. Soda bread is a traditional Irish quick-leavened white bread that is still to this day cooked on a flat griddle pan. Substitute with slices of focaccia.

Serves 2

2 tbsp olive oil

1 onion, finely chopped

1 celery stick, finely chopped

100 g (4 oz) rindless smoked bacon rashers, diced

400 g (14 oz) can chopped tomatoes

300 ml (½ pint) hot chicken stock (from a cube is fine)

1 tbsp tomato purée

FOR THE GARLIC TOASTS

50 g (2 oz) unsalted butter, softened

1 garlic clove, crushed

1 tbsp chopped fresh flat-leaf parsley, plus extra to garnish

1 soda farl, cut into eight slices

salt and freshly ground black pepper

Preheat the grill and heat the oil in a large pan. Add the onion, celery and bacon and cook over a high heat for about 2–3 minutes or until the onion has softened and the bacon is cooked through and lightly golden, stirring occasionally.

Add the chopped tomatoes, chicken stock and tomato purée to the pan, stirring to combine. Bring to a simmer and cook for another minute or two until all the flavours are well combined, stirring occasionally.

Meanwhile, make the garlic toasts. Mix the butter in a bowl with the garlic, parsley and a good pinch of salt, then spread over the soda farl slices. Arrange on a baking sheet, buttered side up and grill for a few minutes until bubbling.

Season the soup and then whiz with a hand blender until smooth. Ladle into warmed bowls and set on plates. Garnish with a sprinkling of parsley and a good grinding of black pepper. Arrange the garlic toasts to the side to serve.

‘ Soda far, soda good ’

Paul Rankin
CHILLED MELON SOUP

This delicate soup makes a wonderful first course in the summer. When buying melons, choose ones that are heavy for their size. A ripe specimen will be slightly soft at the stalk end and perfumed. Try making this with a sweet white wine such as Muscat or Sauternes and omit the sugar.

Serves 2

50 g (2 oz) caster sugar
1 ripe melon (such as Charentais)
50 ml (2 fl oz) dry white wine
small handful fresh basil leaves, plus
    extra tiny sprigs to garnish
good handful ice cubes
½ lemon, pips removed (optional)

Place the caster sugar in a small pan with 120 ml (4 fl oz) of water and heat gently until the sugar has dissolved. Remove from the heat and pour into a jug.

Cut the melon in half and discard the pips, then scoop the flesh into a food processor or liquidizer.

Add the sugar syrup to the food processor with the wine and basil, and then tip in the ice. Blend to a purée and taste, adding a squeeze of the lemon juice if you think it needs it.

Divide the soup between glass bowls and garnish each one with a basil sprig to serve.

Nick Nairn
GAZPACHO

This famous cold soup from Andalucia in Spain is really a blended salad in a bowl. I like to serve it in rustic glass bowls on a hot summer day with whatever is ripe and to hand. For that extra special touch, pop in a couple of ice cubes that have been frozen with tiny herb sprigs.

Serves 2

1 thick slice country-style bread
    (1–2 days old)
1 romero red pepper
½ cucumber
400 g (14 oz) can chopped tomatoes
1 shallot, chopped
1 mild red chilli, seeded and chopped
1 garlic clove, chopped
small handful basil leaves
1 tbsp white wine vinegar
1 tsp caster sugar
handful ice cubes
extra-virgin olive oil, for drizzling
salt and freshly ground black pepper

Remove the crusts from the bread and then roughly chop. Place in a food processor or liquidizer and whiz to breadcrumbs.

Cut the romero pepper in half and remove the seeds, then roughly chop most of the flesh, reserving a small amount that gets finely diced and set aside as garnish. Place in the food processor.

Peel the cucumber, cut in half and discard the seeds, then chop the flesh and add to the food processor with the tomatoes, shallot, chilli, garlic, basil, vinegar and sugar. Tip in the ice cubes and blend to a smooth purée, then season to taste.

Pour the gazpacho into glass bowls and sprinkle in the reserved romero pepper. Add a drizzle of olive oil to each one and serve at once.

James Martin
CHILLED TOMATO AND BASIL SOUP

I like to use fresh plum tomatoes only if they are rich in colour and quite soft.
Otherwise use a 400 g (14 oz) can of plum tomatoes, or try fresh vine-ripened
tomatoes, which normally have a decent flavour and tend to be sold riper.

Serves 2

3 ripe plum tomatoes
1 garlic clove, chopped
2 spring onions, chopped
good handful fresh basil leaves
   (about 7 g (¼ oz) in total)
25 ml (1 fl oz) white wine
½ tsp tomato purée
3 ice cubes
extra-virgin olive oil, for drizzling
salt and freshly ground black pepper
hot French bread and butter, to serve

Cut the tomatoes into quarters and place in a food processor with the
garlic, spring onions and most of the basil, reserving a couple of leaves for
garnish. Add the wine, tomato purée and ice cubes with two tablespoons
of water. Season to taste and blitz for about 30 seconds until smooth.

Pour the tomato and basil soup into chilled bowls and drizzle each one
with a little olive oil. Rip up the remaining basil leaves and scatter on top.
Serve at once with some hot French bread and butter.

James Tanner
PRAWN AND COCONUT BROTH

Very contemporary, easy to make, fragrant and delicious: the perfect soup.
Thailand in a bowl.

Serves 2

1 tbsp sunflower oil
1 shallot, finely diced
1 mild red chilli, seeded and
   finely chopped
1 lemon grass stalk, outer leaves
   removed and core finely chopped
300 ml (½ pint) hot chicken stock
   (from a cube is fine)
120 ml (4 fl oz) coconut milk
100 g (4 oz) raw peeled tiger prawns,
   cleaned
1 baby pak choi, finely shredded
juice ½ lime
small handful torn fresh
   coriander leaves
wafer-thin lime slices, to garnish

Heat the oil in a large pan and gently fry the shallot, chilli and lemon
grass for 1–2 minutes until fragrant.

Pour the stock and coconut milk into the pan and bring to a simmer,
then continue to simmer for 2–3 minutes to allow the flavours to combine.

Add the prawns and pak choi to the coconut mixture and allow to
just warm through. Add the lime juice and coriander leaves, stirring
to combine.

Ladle the broth into warmed bowls and garnish with the lime slices
to serve.

Gino D'Acampo
CREAM OF WATERCRESS SOUP

When watercress is in season and at its best, this is an excellent, almost instant soup. Just don't be tempted to overcook the watercress or it will lose its beautiful, vibrant colour. ▶

Serves 2

4 tbsp double cream
knob unsalted butter
1 garlic clove, finely chopped
300 ml (½ pint) hot vegetable stock
(from a cube is fine)
120 ml (4 fl oz) milk
200 g (7 oz) bunch watercress
good handful fresh flat-leaf
parsley leaves
salt and freshly ground black pepper
fresh chives, to garnish

Lightly whip the cream in a small bowl, then cover with cling film and chill until needed.

Melt the butter in a pan and add the garlic. Cook for 1–2 minutes until softened but not coloured, stirring constantly. Pour the stock into the pan with the milk. Season to taste and cook for a further 2 minutes until the liquid is just beginning to simmer. Trim the bunch of watercress, remove any thick stalks and discoloured leaves, then chop up the remainder.

Add the chopped watercress to the pan with the parsley. Simmer for 1 minute – any longer and the watercress will start to lose its colour. Purée the soup in a food processor or liquidizer and ladle into warmed bowls. Add swirls of the lightly whipped cream and garnish with the chives to serve.

Lesley Waters
MUSHROOM CAPPUCCINO

I like to serve this rich, intensely flavoured soup in cappuccino cups. Just before serving, give the soup a good froth-up with an electric hand blender to lighten the texture.

Serves 2

25 g (1 oz) butter
1 tbsp olive oil
200 g (7 oz) mixed wild mushrooms,
sliced
2 garlic cloves, finely chopped
300 ml (½ pint) hot vegetable stock
(from a cube is fine)
75 ml (3 fl oz) double cream
pinch freshly grated nutmeg
salt and freshly ground black pepper
sliced ciabatta bread, to serve

Heat the butter and oil in a pan. Add the mushrooms and garlic and sauté for 3 minutes until tender. Pour in the stock and bring to the boil, then reduce the heat and simmer gently for 5–6 minutes until the mushrooms are tender and the liquid has slightly reduced.

Add the double cream and nutmeg and season to taste. Using a hand blender, blend until frothy, then divide between large cappuccino cups. Place on saucers with pieces of ciabatta to the side to serve.

Tony Tobin
CHINESE-STYLE CRAB AND SWEETCORN SOUP

This is a super quick version of an old favourite that makes an appearance on every Chinese takeaway menu in the country. If you can't get hold of fresh corn on the cob, use 100 g (4 oz) of frozen sweetcorn kernels instead.

Serves 2

1 corn on the cob
2 tbsp sunflower oil
4 spring onions, finely chopped
2 garlic cloves, finely chopped
300 ml (½ pint) hot chicken stock
    (from a cube is fine)
50 g (2 oz) fresh white crabmeat,
    thawed if frozen
a little sesame oil
salt and freshly ground black pepper

Heat a griddle pan until hot and cook the corn on the cob for 3–4 minutes until the kernels are lightly toasted, turning regularly. Using a sharp knife, cut the toasted sweetcorn kernels off the cob.

Meanwhile, heat the oil in a pan and sauté the spring onions and garlic for 2 minutes until softened but not coloured.

Pour the stock into the pan and bring to the boil, then add the toasted corn and simmer for 4–5 minutes until the sweetcorn is tender.

Stir the crabmeat into the soup until just warmed through and season to taste. Ladle into warmed bowls and drizzle with a little sesame oil to serve.

Ross Burden
CREAMY PEA SOUP WITH PARSLEY CROUTONS

I often make this soup when the cupboards are bare – it's funny how you always have a bag of peas in the freezer. It would also be excellent served chilled on a hot summer's day.

Serves 2

50 g (2 oz) butter
1 small onion, finely chopped
1 thick slice stale white bread,
    crusts removed and cut into
    0.5 cm (¼ in) cubes
1 tsp chopped fresh flat-leaf parsley
200 g (7 oz) frozen peas
300 ml (½ pint) hot chicken or vegetable
    stock (from a cube is fine)
100 ml (3½ fl oz) double cream
salt and freshly ground black pepper

Melt half the butter in a pan and once foaming, tip in the onion. Sweat for 3 minutes until softened but not coloured, stirring occasionally.

Meanwhile, heat the remaining butter in a frying pan. Add the bread cubes and sauté for 6–8 minutes until crisp and golden brown. Season to taste and sprinkle over the parsley, tossing until evenly coated. Drain on kitchen paper.

Add the peas to the onion mixture and cook for another 4 minutes until the peas are tender and cooked through, stirring occasionally.

Pour the stock into the pan with the cream and cook for another minute to warm through, then tip into a food processor or liquidizer and blend until smooth. Season to taste and return to the pan to reheat gently.

Ladle the creamy pea soup into warmed bowls and garnish with the parsley croutons to serve.

Nick Nairn
BEETROOT SOUP

This soup is similar to a Russian borscht, which is traditionally made with beetroot, cabbage and potatoes simmered in beef stock. However, this version has surprising depth of flavour and a wonderful rich colour.

Serves 2

1 tbsp olive oil
1 bunch spring onions, finely chopped
300 ml (½ pint) carton fresh beef stock
dash Worcestershire sauce
400 g (14 oz) jar baby beetroot, drained
   and roughly chopped
2 tbsp soured cream
½ tsp snipped fresh chives
salt and freshly ground black pepper

Heat the olive oil in a pan and sauté the spring onions for 2–3 minutes until softened but not coloured.

Pour the beef stock and Worcestershire sauce into the pan and bring to a simmer, then transfer to a food processor or liquidizer. Add the beetroot and blend until smooth. Season to taste.

Return the soup to a clean pan and allow to just warm through, adding a little water if you think it's too thick.

Divide the soup between warmed bowls and add a spoonful of soured cream to each one. Sprinkle over the chives and serve at once.

James Tanner
CANNELLINI BEAN SOUP WITH SIZZLING CHORIZO

This is one of my 'empty larder' recipes; it requires little preparation and is quickly cooked. The sizzling chorizo makes a delicious topping, which everyone seems to enjoy.

Serves 2

2 tbsp olive oil
knob butter
1 small onion, finely chopped
2 celery sticks, peeled and finely
   chopped
2 garlic cloves, finely chopped
½ tsp chopped fresh thyme
450 ml (¾ pint) hot chicken stock
   (from a cube is fine)
400 g (14 oz) can cannellini beans,
   drained and rinsed
100 g (4 oz) raw chorizo, peeled
   and diced
salt and freshly ground white pepper

Heat half the oil and the butter in a large pan and heat a frying pan. Add the onion, celery and garlic to the pan and cook gently for 2–3 minutes until softened but not coloured.

Stir the thyme into the pan and cook for another 30 seconds and then pour in the stock. Tip in the beans and bring to the boil, then reduce the heat and simmer for another 4–5 minutes until the flavours have combined and the liquid has slightly reduced. Season to taste.

Meanwhile, add the remaining oil to the heated frying pan. Add the chorizo and sauté for 3–4 minutes until sizzling and the chorizo has begun to bleed its colour into the oil.

Blitz the cannellini bean soup with a hand blender until smooth and ladle into warmed bowls. Spoon over the sizzling chorizo and any oil left in the pan to serve.

Brian Turner
CARROT AND CORIANDER SOUP

This is not only cheap and easy to make but has a fantastic colour. For variations, try a tablespoon of freshly grated root ginger instead of the coriander, or a splash of double cream for a more luxurious finish. ▶

Serves 2

1 tbsp olive oil
4 spring onions, finely chopped
2 large carrots (about 350 g (12 oz) in total)
1 tsp clear honey
squeeze of fresh lemon juice
450 ml (¾ pint) hot vegetable or chicken stock (from a cube is fine)
small handful fresh coriander leaves
salt and freshly ground black pepper
extra-virgin olive oil, to garnish
warm focaccia, to serve (optional)

Heat the olive oil in a large pan and sauté the spring onions for a minute or so until softened but not coloured.

Meanwhile, using the grater attachment of a food processor, finely grate the carrots. Add to the pan with the honey and lemon juice, stirring to combine.

Pour the hot stock into the pan and bring to the boil, then boil fast for 5 minutes or until the carrots are tender. Stir in the coriander and blitz with a hand blender until smooth. Season to taste.

Ladle the soup into warm bowls and add a swirl of the extra-virgin olive oil to garnish. Serve at once with warmed focaccia, if liked.

Antony Worrall Thompson
BROCCOLI SOUP WITH BRIE CROSTINI

Impressive enough to grace any sophisticated table, and it can be made in the time it takes your guest to have a drink.

Serves 2

1 tbsp olive oil
1 small onion, finely chopped
450 ml (¾ pint) hot vegetable stock (from a cube is fine)
275 g (10 oz) broccoli florets
1 small French baguette
2 tbsp olive oil
1 garlic clove, halved
100 g (4 oz) ripe Brie, cut into slices
2 tbsp double cream (optional)
1 tbsp chopped fresh flat-leaf parsley
salt and freshly ground black pepper

Preheat the grill. Heat the oil in a pan and pan-fry the onion for 2–3 minutes until softened but not coloured.

Pour the stock into a pan and then tip in the broccoli florets. Bring to the boil, then reduce the heat and simmer for 4–6 minutes until the broccoli is tender but still retains its vibrant colour.

Meanwhile, make the Brie crostini. Cut the baguette into 0.5 cm (¼ in) slices on the diagonal and arrange on the grill rack. Drizzle over the olive oil and season generously. Toast on both sides until lightly golden, then remove from the heat. Rub each piece with garlic, arrange the Brie on top and season with pepper. Flash under the grill until the Brie is bubbling.

Carefully transfer the broccoli and stock mixture to a food processor and season to taste, then whiz to a purée, adding cream if desired. Ladle into warmed bowls set on plates and scatter the parsley on top. Arrange the Brie crostini to the side to serve.

light bites

Paul Rankin
RED PEPPER AND COURGETTE TORTILLA

For a more substantial meal, scatter curds of creamy goat's cheese into the tortilla
and serve with a tumble of Parma ham on top of each tortilla wedge and dressed
salad leaves to the side.

Serves 2–4

1 tbsp olive oil
4 spring onions, finely chopped
1 romero red pepper, halved, seeded
  and thinly sliced
1 small courgette, thinly sliced on
  the diagonal
400 g (14 oz) can cooked baby new
  potatoes, drained and sliced
½ tsp fresh thyme leaves
2 tbsp shredded fresh basil
6 eggs
2 tbsp freshly grated Parmesan
salt and freshly ground black pepper

Preheat the grill to high and heat the oil in a non-stick frying pan. Add the
spring onions, red pepper, courgette and potatoes and sauté for 2–3
minutes until the pepper has softened and the potatoes are heated
through. Stir in the thyme and basil, then season to taste and cook for
another minute.

Meanwhile, lightly beat the eggs in a bowl with a good pinch of seasoning.
Add to the pepper mixture and cook for another few minutes, stirring very
gently until the eggs begin to set. Spread the mixture out evenly over the
pan and press down very gently with a fish slice until the bottom of the
tortilla is set.

Sprinkle over the Parmesan and place the tortilla directly under the grill
for another minute or two until glazed and slightly puffed. Turn out onto a
warm plate and cut into wedges to serve.

'Nice tortilla, tortilla nice!'

Nick Nairn
FLATBREAD PIZZA

If you think making a pizza from scratch takes loads of time and effort kneading and tossing, then have a go at this super-quick version … *Mamma mia* – you're in for a treat. ▶

Serves 1–2

150 g (5 oz) self-raising flour, plus
    extra for dusting
pinch salt
2 tbsp olive oil, plus extra for drizzling
1 small green pepper, halved, seeded
    and thinly sliced
50 g (2 oz) tiny cherry tomatoes, halved
100 g (4 oz) ball buffalo mozzarella,
    roughly torn into pieces
handful small basil leaves

Preheat the oven to 220°C/425°F/Gas 7 and heat a large ovenproof frying pan. Place the flour in a bowl with a pinch of salt. Make a well in the centre and whisk in about 4 tablespoons of water until the mixture just binds together. Drizzle in the olive oil and work the ingredients together with your hands to make a soft dough.

On a lightly floured work surface, roll out the dough into a circle that will fit the bottom of the frying pan comfortably. Add to the heated frying pan and, while the underneath is cooking, use a blowtorch to cook the top for 2 minutes until puffed up.

Then flip the base over and continue to cook for another minute or two, while you scatter the green pepper and cherry tomatoes on top. Interweave with the mozzarella and finish with the basil leaves. Drizzle over a little olive oil, transfer to the oven and bake for 5 minutes or so until the mozzarella has melted and the base is cooked through.

Remove the pizza from the oven. Transfer to a large flat plate and cut into slices to serve.

Tony Tobin
CREAMY GARLIC MUSHROOMS ON TOAST

I was lucky enough to have some big velvet-gilled flat mushrooms for this dish, but all manner of mushrooms respond well to being quickly fried and finished with a splash of cream.

Serves 2

1 tbsp olive oil
knob butter
1 garlic clove, finely chopped
2 large flat mushrooms, sliced
2 thick slices sourdough bread
good splash Madeira
85 ml (3 fl oz) double cream
1 tbsp shredded fresh basil
salt and freshly ground black pepper

Preheat the grill to high and heat a large frying pan. Add the oil and butter to the pan and once the butter stops foaming, tip in the garlic and sauté for 20 seconds without colouring. Add the mushrooms and continue to sauté for 3–4 minutes until tender and all the liquid has evaporated. Season to taste.

Meanwhile, toast the sourdough slices on both sides under the hot grill.

Pour the Madeira over the mushrooms. As soon as it has evaporated, drizzle in the cream, then allow to bubble down and reduce a little.

Place the toasted sourdough on warm plates and spoon the creamy mushrooms on top. Scatter over the basil and serve at once.

PORK SPRING ROLLS WITH CHINESE DIPPING SAUCE

The packet of stir-fried vegetables I was given in this quickie bag contained shredded pak choi, sliced baby corn, coarsely grated carrot and bean sprouts, but you could use any selection you fancy.

Serves 2

sunflower oil, for cooking
1 garlic clove, finely chopped
1 tsp freshly grated root ginger
100 g (4 oz) lean minced pork
25 g (1 oz) prepared stir-fry
   vegetables (from a packet)
dash sesame oil
1 tsp dark soy sauce
10 spring roll or wonton wrappers
   (10 cm/4 in), thawed if frozen
1 egg yolk beaten with 2 tbsp water
salt and freshly ground black pepper

FOR THE CHINESE DIPPING SAUCE
1 tbsp sesame oil
2 tsp tomato ketchup
few drops Tabasco sauce
1 tsp dark soy sauce
good pinch dried crushed chillies
1 tbsp chopped fresh coriander

Preheat a deep-fat fryer or fill a flat-bottomed wok one-third full with oil and heat to 190°C/375°F. If you don't have a thermometer, the oil should be hot enough so that when a bread cube is added, it browns in 40 seconds.

Heat one tablespoon of the sunflower oil in a non-stick frying pan and stir-fry the garlic, ginger, pork and seasoning for a couple of minutes until the pork is sealed and lightly browned.

Add the stir-fry vegetables with the sesame oil and soy sauce and continue to stir-fry for another 2–3 minutes until the pork is cooked through and the vegetables are still crunchy. Tip out onto a baking sheet and spread out to allow the mixture to cool as quickly as possible.

Place a heaped tablespoon near one of the corners of a spring roll or wonton wrapper. Pull over the corner to enclose the filling completely, then fold in the two sides, brush with the egg yolk mixture to seal and roll up like a cigar. Repeat until you have ten spring rolls in total.

Deep-fry the spring rolls for 1–2 minutes until crisp and golden brown. Drain well on kitchen paper.

Meanwhile, make the Chinese dipping sauce. Place all the ingredients in a bowl and whisk to combine.

Arrange the pork spring rolls on warmed plates. Divide the sauce between individual dipping bowls and set to the side of each plate to serve.

Gino D'Acampo
SESAME PRAWN TOASTS WITH CUCUMBER DIPPING SAUCE

You can eat these toasts as starters, snacks or canapés, depending on your mood.
Try to use bread that's a day or two old so that it has dried out slightly.

Serves 2

sunflower oil, for deep-frying
150 g (5 oz) raw peeled tiger prawns,
   cleaned
1 spring onion, chopped
1 tsp freshly grated root ginger
½ mild red chilli, seeded and
   finely chopped
1 tbsp chopped fresh coriander
½ tsp cornflour
1 small egg white
3 slices white bread
1 tbsp sesame seeds

FOR THE CUCUMBER DIPPING SAUCE

2 tbsp rice wine vinegar
1 tbsp caster sugar
½ small cucumber, peeled, halved,
   seeded and finely chopped
¼ mild red chilli, seeded and
   thinly sliced
salt and freshly ground black pepper

Preheat a deep-fat fryer or fill a deep-sided pan one-third full with oil and heat to 180°F/350F. If you don't have a thermometer, the oil should be hot enough so that when a bread cube is added, it browns in 60 seconds.

To make the cucumber dipping sauce, place the vinegar in a bowl and stir in the sugar and a pinch of salt to dissolve. Add the cucumber and chilli and toss to coat. Cover with cling film and set aside for at least 5 minutes.

Place the prawns in a food processor with the spring onion, ginger, chilli, coriander, cornflour, egg white and seasoning. Blitz until well combined and then spread over the slices of bread. Sprinkle each slice of bread with a teaspoon of sesame seeds and then cut off the crusts.

Deep-fry the toasts for 1–1½ minutes on each side until golden brown. Drain well on kitchen paper and cut each slice into four triangles. Arrange the prawn toasts on warmed plates with individual bowls of the cucumber dipping sauce to serve.

light bites

45

James Tanner
GRATIN MUSSELS

Food trends come and go but this recipe has stood the test of time. ◄

Serves 2

24 large fresh mussels, cleaned
glug dry white wine
25 g (1 oz) unsalted butter
1 garlic clove, crushed
2 slices day-old white bread, crusts
 removed and diced
pinch finely diced bird's-eye red chilli
small handful fresh flat-leaf
 parsley leaves
salt and freshly ground black pepper
lemon wedges, to serve

Preheat the grill and heat a large pan until hot. Add the mussels with the wine and cover tightly. Cook for 3–4 minutes, shaking the pan halfway through. All the mussels should now have opened – discard any that do not.

Meanwhile, melt the butter in a small pan and gently sauté the garlic for 1 minute without colouring. Tip into a food processor or liquidizer.

Drain the mussels through a colander and allow to cool for a minute or two.

Add the bread to the food processor with the chilli and parsley, then blitz to fine crumbs. Season to taste.

Discard the empty half shells from the mussels. Arrange the mussels in a shallow baking tin and spoon the breadcrumbs on top to cover completely. Put under the grill for 2 minutes until crisp and lightly golden. Arrange the gratin mussels on warmed plates with lemon wedges to garnish.

James Martin
SPINACH AND PARMESAN FILO TARTS

A glamorous snack that is deceptively easy; the cases are quickly made using filo pastry. If you don't have cooking rings, a four-hole Yorkshire pudding tin is a useful substitute.

Serves 2

4 sheets filo pastry, thawed if frozen
50 g (2 oz) butter, melted
225 g (8 oz) baby spinach leaves
225 ml (8 fl oz) double cream
2 egg yolks
100 g (4 oz) freshly grated Parmesan
50 g (2 oz) pine nuts
salt and freshly ground black pepper

Preheat the oven to 220°C/425°F/Gas 7. Place two 10 cm (4 in) metal cooking rings on a large non-stick baking sheet. Cut down each filo sheet into a square of approximately 15 cm (6 in). Brush with melted butter and layer two in each ring at an angle to each other to form a crown. Press down firmly into the ring and bake for 2–3 minutes until crisp and lightly golden.

Meanwhile, put the spinach and remaining butter in a small pan and wilt, draining off any excess liquid. Place the cream, egg yolks and Parmesan in a bowl and whisk to combine. Season to taste and fold in the spinach.

Remove the filo cases from the oven and divide the spinach mixture between them. Bake for another 4–5 minutes until the tarts are just set and the filo is golden brown.

Meanwhile, toast the pine nuts in a dry frying pan for a few minutes, tossing to ensure they cook evenly. Remove the cooked tarts from the oven, transfer to warmed plates and scatter over the toasted pine nuts to serve.

light bites

Brian Turner
HUMMUS WITH GRIDDLED APRICOT FLATBREAD

These flatbreads take no time at all to prepare and are just as good as any you will have ever tasted. Use them to mop up the hummus or serve them with your favourite curry as part of an Indian feast.

Serves 2

1 tbsp sesame seeds

400 g (14 oz) can chickpeas, drained and rinsed

1 small garlic clove, crushed

2 tbsp freshly squeezed lemon juice

1 tbsp chopped fresh coriander

100–120 ml (3½–4 fl oz) olive oil, plus extra to serve

FOR THE GRIDDLED APRICOT FLATBREAD

4 spring onions, finely chopped

½ tsp medium curry powder

100 g (4 oz) plain flour

1 tsp baking powder

finely grated rind of 1 lemon

4 ready-to-eat dried apricots, finely chopped

olive oil, for drizzling

salt and freshly ground black pepper

To make the flatbread, heat a large flat griddle pan. Mix together the spring onions, curry powder, flour, baking powder, lemon rind and apricots in a large bowl. Season to taste. Make a well in the centre and gradually add about 4 tablespoons of water to make a soft dough.

Turn the dough out onto a lightly floured surface and knead gently until rounded and smooth. Cut into two pieces and roll each one out into an oval shape, then drizzle with a little olive oil. Add to the heated flat griddle pan and cook for 2–3 minutes on each side until cooked through and lightly golden, drizzling the other side with a little more olive oil if necessary.

Meanwhile, to make the hummus, toast the sesame seeds in a small frying pan, then tip into a food processor. Add the chickpeas, garlic, lemon juice and coriander and whiz until smooth. With the machine still running, gradually add enough olive oil to make a smooth creamy dip. Season to taste and spoon into a bowl. Drizzle with a little more olive oil and set on a large plate. When the flatbreads are cooked, cut them into fingers and pile up alongside the hummus to serve.

Ross Burden
PARMA HAM BRUSCHETTA WITH TOMATO DRESSING

The salty flavour of the Parma ham goes perfectly with the fresh herbs and zingy tomato dressing.

Serves 2

6 slices French bread, cut on
  the diagonal
2 tbsp olive oil
2 tbsp shredded fresh basil
2 tbsp chopped fresh flat-leaf parsley
juice ½ lemon
6 thin slices Parma ham
25 g (1 oz) wild rocket

FOR THE TOMATO DRESSING

4 tbsp extra-virgin olive oil
1 garlic clove, finely chopped
3 ripe tomatoes, peeled, seeded
  and chopped
1 tsp tomato purée
1 tbsp balsamic vinegar
dash Tabasco sauce
salt and freshly ground black pepper

To make the tomato dressing, heat one tablespoon of the olive oil in a frying pan and sauté the garlic for 30 seconds to 1 minute, until softened but not coloured. Tip into a mini food processor and add the remaining olive oil, the tomatoes, tomato purée, balsamic vinegar and Tabasco. Blend until smooth, then season to taste. Pour into a small jug or bowl and set aside until needed.

Heat a griddle pan until smoking hot. Drizzle the French bread slices with one tablespoon of the olive oil and add to the pan. Cook for 1–2 minutes on each side until nicely marked and crisp.

Meanwhile, place the herbs in a bowl with the lemon juice and remaining olive oil. Toss well to coat and season with pepper. Spoon a little of the herb mixture onto the end of each slice of Parma ham and roughly fold over to enclose.

Scatter a little rocket on each piece of crostini and arrange the flavoured Parma ham on top. Divide between plates, or use a platter, and drizzle a little of the tomato dressing over each bruschetta before serving.

‘ Things can only get bruschetta ’

Lesley Waters
EGGS BENEDICT ROYALE

The secret to a trouble-free beurre blanc is to keep the sauce at the right temperature. To test it, stick your finger in – the sauce should feel warm, not hot. ▶

Serves 2

½ tsp white wine vinegar
2 large eggs
1 soft white muffin, halved
olive oil, for cooking
4 slices smoked salmon
    (about 100 g (4 oz) in total)

FOR THE BEURRE BLANC

100 ml (3½ fl oz) double cream
25 g (1 oz) unsalted butter
juice ½ lemon
2 tsp Dijon mustard
dash Tabasco sauce
salt and freshly ground black pepper
fresh dill sprigs, to garnish

Preheat the grill. To make the beurre blanc, place the cream, butter, lemon juice, mustard and Tabasco in a small pan. Heat for 3–4 minutes, whisking until the sauce is thick and glossy. Season to taste and keep it warm.

Meanwhile, heat a large pan of boiling water with the vinegar. When the water is bubbling, break the eggs in, then move the pan to the edge of the heat and simmer gently for 3 minutes.

Toast the muffin halves for 3–4 minutes under the hot grill until lightly golden. Heat a non-stick frying pan, add a thin film of oil and lightly sear the smoked salmon for up to 1 minute on each side.

Remove the poached eggs with a slotted spoon, drain on kitchen paper and trim down any ragged edges. Put a muffin half on each of two warmed plates and arrange the salmon on top. Top with a poached egg and either spoon over the beurre blanc or serve it on the side. Garnish with dill and black pepper and serve at once.

Gino D'Acampo
CRUNCHY FISH FINGERS WITH YOGHURT DIP

My children love these fish fingers, which are much healthier and better-tasting than shop-bought.

Serves 2

sunflower oil, for deep-frying
50 g (2 oz) toasted natural breadcrumbs
2 tbsp freshly grated Parmesan
2 eggs
2 tbsp milk
25 g (1 oz) seasoned flour
225 g (8 oz) lemon sole fillets

FOR THE CHILLI-CHIVE YOGHURT DIP

100 g (4 oz) Greek yoghurt
2 tbsp snipped fresh chives
squeeze lime juice
2 tbsp sweet chilli sauce
salt and freshly ground black pepper
lime wedges, to garnish

Preheat a deep-fat fryer or fill a deep-sided pan one-third full with oil and heat to 180°F/350°F. If you don't have a thermometer, the oil should be hot enough so that when a bread cube is added, it browns in 60 seconds.

Place the breadcrumbs and Parmesan in a shallow dish, season and mix well. Beat the eggs and milk together in a separate shallow dish. Put the seasoned flour on a flat plate. Cut the lemon sole into strips, then dust in the flour, tip into the egg and finally roll in the breadcrumbs. Repeat with the egg and breadcrumbs to double-coat each piece. Deep-fry in batches for 2–3 minutes until cooked through and golden brown. Drain on kitchen paper and keep warm.

To make the dip, combine the yoghurt, chives and lime juice and season well. Divide between dipping bowls and spoon a layer of the sweet chilli sauce on top. Pile the crunchy fish fingers onto warmed plates and serve with a bowl of the chilli-chive yoghurt dip and lime wedges to the side.

salads

James Martin
SUN-BLUSHED TOMATO SALAD WITH BACON AND POACHED EGG

If time allows, the poached eggs can be cooked in advance and plunged into a bowl of iced cold water until needed, then you just slip them back into hot salted water when you are ready to serve.

Serves 2

1 ciabatta loaf
5 tbsp olive oil, plus extra for brushing
1 small red onion, sliced
75 g (3 oz) rindless streaky bacon rashers, chopped
1 garlic clove, chopped
50 g (2 oz) cambozola cheese, rind removed, diced
juice ½ lemon
3 tbsp milk
dash white wine vinegar
2 large eggs
50 g (2 oz) sun-blushed tomatoes, roughly chopped
1 tbsp chopped fresh flat-leaf parsley
1 tbsp snipped fresh chives
salt and freshly ground black pepper

Preheat the oven to 200°C/400°F/Gas 6 and heat a griddle pan until searing hot. Cut the crusts off the ciabatta loaf and then cut into 1 cm (½ in) cubes. Toss half with two tablespoons of the olive oil and spread out in a baking tin. Season to taste and cook for about 8 minutes until lightly golden, tossing occasionally to ensure they cook evenly. Reserve the remainder of the bread cubes for the dressing.

Brush the griddle pan with a little oil and add the onion and bacon. Cook for 3–4 minutes until cooked through and lightly charred, turning regularly.

Place the rest of the bread cubes in a food processor to make the dressing – you should have about 75 g (3 oz) in total. Whiz until fine breadcrumbs have formed, then add the remaining three tablespoons of olive oil with the garlic, cambozola, lemon juice and milk and blend until smooth. Season to taste.

Heat a large pan of boiling water with the vinegar. When the water is bubbling, break the eggs into the water, then move the pan to the edge of the heat and simmer gently for 3 minutes. Remove each poached egg with a slotted spoon and quickly trim down any ragged edges.

Place the char-grilled bacon and onion in a large bowl with the sun-blushed tomatoes, parsley, chives and croutons. Toss with enough of the dressing to lightly coat and season to taste. Arrange the salad on plates and top each one with a poached egg to serve.

salads

55

‘The yolk's on him’

Gino D'Acampo
ORIENTAL-STYLE SESAME DUCK SALAD

This has to be one of my favourite ways of cooking duck. Obviously the duck here is served quite pink due to time constraints, but you could always increase the time by a couple of minutes if you prefer yours more well done.

Serves 2

1 small duck breast fillet, well trimmed
   (about 100 g (4 oz) in total)
1 tbsp olive oil
2 tbsp clear honey
1 tbsp toasted sesame seeds
100 g (4 oz) baby spinach leaves

FOR THE DRESSING
1 tbsp olive oil
1 tsp sesame oil
1 tbsp toasted sesame seeds
1 tsp dark soy sauce
juice ½ lime
1 tsp clear honey
1 tbsp chopped fresh flat-leaf parsley
salt and freshly ground black pepper

Heat a heavy-based ovenproof frying pan. Score the skin on the duck breast and rub all over with the olive oil. Add to the pan, skin-side down, and cook for 5 minutes until the skin is golden brown.

To make the dressing, place the olive oil in a bowl with the sesame oil, sesame seeds, soy sauce, lime juice, honey and parsley. Whisk until well combined.

Pour off the excess fat produced by the duck, then turn over and drizzle the honey and the sesame seeds on top. Transfer to the oven and cook for another 2–3 minutes until just tender. Remove from the oven and leave to rest as long as time allows, then slice into thin strips on the diagonal.

Add the spinach to the dressing, season to taste and toss until all the leaves are well coated. Arrange the duck slices in a fan shape in the centre of each plate and divide the salad between them to serve.

Brian Turner
TOMATO SALAD WITH ROASTED RED PEPPERS

This great-looking salad would be perfect as a meal on its own with a chunk of crusty bread, or as part of a barbecue spread.

Serves 2

2 ripe beef tomatoes, thinly sliced
100 g (4 oz) roasted red peppers from a jar, drained with 2 tbsp of the oil reserved
50 g (2 oz) pitted black olives
handful fresh basil leaves, shredded
½ tsp balsamic vinegar
salt and freshly ground black pepper

Arrange the beef tomatoes in a single layer on the base of a large plate.

Mix together the roasted red peppers, olives and basil in a bowl and then scatter on top of the tomatoes. Drizzle the roasted red pepper oil on top with the balsamic vinegar. Add a good grinding of pepper and a sprinkling of salt. Serve at once.

Antony Worrall Thompson
ROCKET, RADICCHIO AND PINE NUT SALAD WITH PARMESAN SHAVINGS

Sometimes the simplest salads work the best. The sharp, contrasting flavours of the peppery rocket, bitter radicchio, Parmesan and toasted nuts work a treat.

Serves 2–4

2 tbsp pine nuts
1 small head radicchio
25 g (1 oz) rocket leaves
1½ tsp balsamic vinegar
1 tsp freshly squeezed lemon juice
3 tbsp extra-virgin olive oil
25 g (1 oz) piece Parmesan (Parmigiano Reggiano or Grana Padano)
salt and freshly ground black pepper

Toast the pine nuts in a dry frying pan for 6–8 minutes, tossing occasionally to ensure that they cook evenly. Pour onto a flat plate and spread out to cool.

Meanwhile, cut the radicchio into quarters and remove the white central core; discard. Cut each piece crossways into strips that are roughly the same size as the rocket leaves. Place in a large bowl with the rocket.

Mix the balsamic vinegar with the lemon juice in a small bowl. Whisk in the olive oil and season to taste.

Using a potato peeler, pare the Parmesan into thin shavings.

Add the cooled pine nuts to the rocket mixture and pour over enough of the dressing to barely coat the leaves, tossing to combine. Divide between plates and scatter over the Parmesan shavings to serve.

Rocket science

Ross Burden
PANZANELLA

This is a variation on a very old recipe that has its origins in Tuscany, where it was traditional to soak the bread in pure seawater to give a distinctive taste of the sea.

Serves 2

¼ loaf rustic white bread
  (about 100 g (4 oz) in total)
1–2 tbsp olive oil
75 g (3 oz) pitted black olives
75 g (3 oz) cherry tomatoes, halved
25 g (1 oz) fresh flat-leaf parsley leaves
handful pecorino shavings

FOR THE DRESSING

25 g (1 oz) cherry tomatoes
1 tsp tomato purée
1 tbsp red wine vinegar
3 tbsp extra-virgin olive oil
salt and freshly ground black pepper

Preheat the oven to 200°C/400°F/Gas 6. Cut the bread into pieces roughly 1 cm (½ in) across. Place in a baking tin and drizzle with enough of the olive oil to barely coat. Bake for about 8 minutes until crisp and golden brown, tossing occasionally for even cooking.

To make the dressing, place the cherry tomatoes in a mini food processor with the tomato purée, vinegar and olive oil. Blitz to a purée and season to taste. Pour into a small jug and set aside.

Place the olives, cherry tomatoes and parsley in a large bowl. Add the croutons, tossing to combine, then drizzle in enough dressing to coat the salad evenly. Divide between plates and scatter over the pecorino shavings to serve.

Lesley Waters
SEARED GRAVADLAX AND HERB SALAD WITH HORSERADISH DRESSING

The horseradish dressing is easy to prepare and keeps for several weeks in the fridge. I store mine in a plastic squeezy bottle, which makes it perfect for instant 'drizzling' round the edges of the plates.

Serves 2

about 2 tbsp olive oil
4 slices gravadlax
75 g (3 oz) mixed herb salad
½ lemon, pips removed

FOR THE HORSERADISH DRESSING

2 tbsp creamed horseradish
100 ml (3½ fl oz) olive oil
squeeze lemon juice
1 tbsp snipped fresh chives
freshly ground black pepper

Heat a large griddle pan. To make the dressing, whisk the creamed horseradish into the olive oil in a small bowl. Stir in the lemon juice to taste with the chives and season with pepper.

Brush the heated griddle pan with one tablespoon of the olive oil and then add the slices of gravadlax. Char-grill for a minute or so on each side.

Place the herb salad in a bowl and dress with the remaining olive oil and enough lemon juice to barely coat the leaves. Divide between plates and top with the seared gravadlax. Add a squeeze of lemon juice, drizzle over the horseradish dressing and serve at once.

Tony Tobin
PEAR AND WALNUT SALAD
WITH GOAT'S CHEESE

Numerous salad-leaf combinations are available in supermarkets. A garden salad with peppery watercress works well in this dish. If your walnuts aren't very fresh, lightly toast them for a much better result. ◄

Serves 2

2 x 50 g (2 oz) goat's cheese slices

2 tbsp seasoned flour

1 tbsp olive oil

50 g (2 oz) walnut halves,
   roughly chopped

1 tsp wholegrain mustard

1 large ripe pear

75 g (3 oz) mixed salad leaves

1 tbsp extra-virgin olive oil

1 tsp white wine vinegar

salt and freshly ground black pepper

Heat a non-stick frying pan. Coat the goat's cheese in the seasoned flour, shaking off any excess. Add the olive oil to the heated frying pan and then add the coated goat's cheese. Cook over a high heat for 1 minute on each side until crisp and lightly golden.

Place the walnuts and wholegrain mustard in a large bowl and combine well. Cut the pear into quarters, remove the core and chop into small pieces. Add to the bowl, along with the salad leaves.

Dress the pear and walnut salad with enough of the extra-virgin olive oil and vinegar to barely coat the leaves. Season to taste. Divide most of the salad between plates, top each one with a piece of the fried goat's cheese and finish off with the remaining salad to serve.

Nick Nairn
ORANGE, WATERCRESS AND MELON SALAD

This dish is dedicated to those who think salads are boring. Packed with fantastic flavours and textures, it is a taste sensation. Pickled walnuts are delicacies from England's West Country, traditionally made from green walnuts picked in July.

Serves 2

1 ripe melon, halved, seeded and
   flesh diced (Charentais)

6 small vine tomatoes, quartered

small handful fresh flat-leaf
   parsley leaves

small handful fresh torn basil leaves

2 tbsp snipped fresh chives

1 tsp balsamic vinegar

juice 1 lemon

4 pickled walnuts, sliced

1 orange, cut into segments

100 g (4 oz) watercress, well
   picked over

extra-virgin olive oil, for drizzling

salt and freshly ground black pepper

Place the melon, tomatoes and herbs in a bowl and mix lightly to combine.

Place the balsamic vinegar, lemon juice, pickled walnuts and orange segments in a separate bowl and toss gently to combine, then fold into the melon and tomato mixture.

Arrange the watercress on a platter and arrange the lemon and tomato mixture on top. Drizzle with the olive oil and season to taste. Serve at once.

salads

Lesley Waters
CORONATION-STYLE TURKEY WITH PARSNIP CHIPS

This recipe is a variation on a classic. You can add wafer-thin slices of cucumber and finely sliced spring onions to the shredded lettuce if you've got them to hand.

Serves 2

3 tbsp Greek yoghurt

2 tbsp mayonnaise

1 tsp mild curry paste or Thai red curry paste

1 garlic clove, crushed

finely grated rind and juice ½ lemon

1 tbsp chopped fresh coriander

225 g (8 oz) cooked turkey breast, shredded

4 ready-to-eat apricots, very finely diced

1 little Gem lettuce

FOR THE PARSNIP CRISPS

sunflower oil, for deep-frying

1 parsnip

1 tbsp plain flour

good pinch curry powder

Maldon sea salt and freshly ground black pepper

chopped fresh flat-leaf parsley, to garnish

To make the parsnip crisps, preheat a deep-fat fryer or fill a deep-sided pan one-third full with oil and heat to 190°F/375°F. If you don't have a thermometer, the oil should be hot enough so that when a bread cube is added, it browns in 40 seconds.

Cut the parsnip into wafer-thin slices with a mandolin or vegetable peeler. Place the flour on a plate and season generously, then add the curry powder and mix to combine. Dust batches of the parsnips in the flour, shaking off any excess, and deep-fry for 1–2 minutes until crisp and lightly golden. Drain well on kitchen paper and repeat until all the crisps are cooked. Pile into a warm bowl and season with salt.

Place the Greek yoghurt in a bowl with the mayonnaise, curry paste, garlic, lemon rind and juice and coriander. Stir until well combined.

Fold the turkey into the Greek yoghurt mixture with the apricots and season to taste.

Spoon the coronation-style turkey into the centre of a small platter. Shred the lettuce and arrange round the edge. Garnish with the parsley and serve at once with the bowl of parsnip crisps.

Gino D'Acampo
SMOKED CHICKEN CAESAR SALAD

This is a quick version of probably the most famous salad in the world. It would be perfect in small portions as a starter, and also excellent as a lunch or light supper dish.

Serves 2

2 thick slices country style bread
4 tbsp olive oil
1 garlic clove, crushed
4 tbsp mayonnaise
squeeze lemon juice
1 tsp Dijon mustard
few drops Tabasco sauce
4 anchovy fillets, crushed to a paste
   (canned or from a jar)
50 g (2 oz) freshly grated Parmesan
1 cos lettuce
100 g (4 oz) smoked chicken breast,
   skinned and shredded
1 tbsp chopped fresh flat-leaf parsley
salt and freshly ground black pepper

To make the croutons, heat a large frying pan. Remove the crusts from the bread and cut into 1 cm (½ in) cubes. Place in a bowl and add half the olive oil. Season generously and toss until well combined. Tip into the heated frying pan and sauté for 6–8 minutes until crisp and golden brown. Drain well on kitchen paper.

To make the dressing, place the remaining two tablespoons of olive oil in a small bowl with the garlic, mayonnaise, lemon juice, mustard, Tabasco, anchovies and half of the Parmesan, then beat until well combined. Season to taste.

Remove and discard any damaged leaves from the cos lettuce, then break the remaining bigger outer leaves roughly, keeping the smaller inside ones whole. Toss with the dressing and the shredded smoked chicken. Arrange in the centre of each plate and scatter over the croutons, parsley and remaining Parmesan to serve.

Phil Vickery

WARM CHORIZO AND CHICKPEA SALAD WITH ROASTED RED PEPPERS

This Middle Eastern-inspired salad is a meal on its own. The flavour combination worked so well that I have made it at home a couple of times since the show. ▶

Serves 2

4 mini white pitta breads
olive oil, for cooking
3 small raw chorizo sausages, thinly sliced on the diagonal
400 g (14 oz) can chickpeas, drained and rinsed
2 roasted peppers, drained and sliced into strips (from a jar, preserved in oil)
squeeze lemon juice
2 tbsp roughly chopped fresh coriander
2 tbsp roughly chopped fresh flat-leaf parsley
2–3 tbsp extra-virgin olive oil
salt and freshly ground black pepper

Heat a griddle pan until very hot and heat a frying pan. Brush both sides of the pitta breads with a little oil and char-grill for a minute or so on each side. Cut into strips on the diagonal and place in a large bowl.

Add the chorizo to the heated frying pan and cook for 3–4 minutes until its oil begins to ooze out, turning occasionally. Add the contents of the pan to the pitta bread with the chickpeas and roasted peppers.

Add the lemon juice to the salad mixture and then fold in the herbs with a good glug of extra-virgin olive oil. Season to taste. Tip onto a warmed platter and serve immediately.

James Tanner

WARM COUSCOUS SALAD

This dish is full of contemporary flavours and textures. It is just as good cold and would make wonderful picnic food, or serve it warm alongside grilled fish fillets marinated in chilli oil.

Serves 2

100 g (4 oz) couscous
4 tbsp extra-virgin olive oil
juice ½ lemon
2 shallots, finely chopped
100 g (4 oz) wild mushrooms, chopped
1 ripe red tomato, halved, seeded and diced
1 ripe yellow tomato, halved, seeded and diced
75 g (3 oz) artichoke hearts preserved in olive oil, drained and chopped
2 tbsp roughly chopped mixed fresh herbs (such as basil, flat-leaf parsley and chives)
salt and freshly ground black pepper

Place the couscous in a large bowl and drizzle over two tablespoons of the olive oil with the lemon juice, stirring gently. Pour over 120 ml (4 fl oz) of boiling water, then stir well, cover and leave to stand for 5 minutes.

Meanwhile, heat the remaining olive oil in a frying pan. Add the shallots and sauté for 1–2 minutes until tender. Add the wild mushrooms and cook for 2–3 minutes more until tender. Add the tomatoes and artichokes and cook for another minute or so until heated through but the tomatoes still hold their shape. Remove from the heat and season to taste.

Gently separate the couscous grains with a fork. Season to taste and place in a pan to reheat gently. Fold in the vegetable mixture with the herbs and divide between warmed plates to serve.

Paul Rankin
THAI CHICKEN SALAD WITH GLASS NOODLES

This has to be one of my favourite salads. It's beautifully fragrant and perfect for a light supper. Try adding a couple of handfuls of small crisp salad leaves as a variation.

Serves 2

100 g (4 oz) rice vermicelli
1 small red onion, thinly sliced
1 large cooked chicken breast
small bunch fresh coriander
handful fresh mint leaves
½ small red pepper, seeded and cut into fine strips
4 tbsp roughly chopped peanuts

FOR THE DRESSING

1 tsp caster sugar
2 tbsp dark soy sauce
1 tbsp sweet chilli sauce
juice 1 lime
4 tbsp sunflower oil

Place the rice vermicelli in a large bowl and cover with boiling water. Leave for about 5 minutes until softened, or follow packet instructions. Place the red onion in a bowl of iced water for 2–3 minutes; this will make the onion crisp and mellow out the flavour a little.

Remove the skin from the chicken breast and then strip off the flesh from the bones before chopping finely. Set aside.

To make the dressing, dissolve the sugar in the soy sauce in a small bowl and then whisk in the sweet chilli sauce, lime juice and sunflower oil.

Drain both the vermicelli and red onion well and place in a large bowl. Tear the coriander and mint leaves away from the stalks and add to the bowl along with the red pepper.

Add the dressing and chicken to the salad, tossing gently with your hands until well combined. Divide between plates, scatter over the peanuts and serve at once.

Brian Turner
SMOKED DUCK WITH POTATO SALAD WITH BEETROOT RELISH

This salad takes no time at all to prepare and is ideal for a sophisticated eating-out-at-home experience. Look out for packets of smoked duck breasts in good supermarkets and delicatessens.

Serves 2

175 g (6 oz) baby new potatoes, scrubbed
3 tbsp extra-virgin olive oil
juice ½ lemon
1 tbsp snipped fresh chives
40 g (1½ oz) lamb's lettuce
100 g (4 oz) smoked duck breast, cut into thin slices

FOR THE BEETROOT RELISH
4 cooked baby beetroot, drained (from a jar)
2 spring onions, finely chopped
1 tsp tiny fresh dill sprigs
pinch sugar
salt and freshly ground black pepper

Cut the new potatoes into slices and cook in a pan of boiling salted water for about 8 minutes or until tender.

To make the beetroot relish, finely chop the beetroot and mix with the spring onion, dill and sugar in a bowl until well combined. Season with pepper.

Place the olive oil, lemon juice and chives in a large bowl. When the potatoes are cooked, drain well and then tip into the bowl, tossing until evenly coated. Season to taste, then quickly fold in the lamb's lettuce and divide between plates.

Arrange the smoked duck on top in a fan shape and add small mounds of the beetroot relish round the edge of the plate to serve.

‘I relish you, be true to me’

salads

67

on the side

Phil Vickery

ONION RINGS WITH SWEET AND SOUR DIP

For me, there's nothing nicer than a tender steak served with a huge pile of these crispy onion rings and a tangy dipping sauce. The onion rings are also great with char-grilled burgers or sticky barbecued ribs.

Serves 2

sunflower oil, for deep-frying
1 red onion
100 g (4 oz) self-raising flour
200 ml (7 fl oz) sparkling water

FOR THE SWEET AND SOUR DIP
100 g (4 oz) ricotta cheese
2 tbsp tomato ketchup
1 tbsp snipped fresh chives
½ tsp Tabasco sauce
½ tsp Worcestershire sauce
salt and freshly ground black pepper

Preheat a deep-fat fryer or fill a deep-sided pan one-third full with oil and heat to 190°C/375°F. If you don't have a thermometer, the oil should be hot enough so that when a bread cube is added, it browns in 40 seconds.

Peel the onion and slice into 1 cm (½ in) slices, then separate into rings. Place the flour in a bowl and make a well in the centre. Pour in the sparkling water and quickly whisk into the flour until you have achieved a smooth batter. Season to taste.

Dip the onion rings into the batter, gently shaking off any excess, then deep-fry for 2–3 minutes until crisp and golden brown. Drain on kitchen paper.

Meanwhile, make the sweet and sour dip. Place the ricotta cheese in a bowl with the tomato ketchup, chives, Tabasco and Worcestershire sauce. Season to taste and mix until well combined. Transfer to a small bowl set on a warmed plate. Pile up the hot onion rings round the sweet and sour dip and serve immediately.

❝Love at first bite❞

on the side

69

Antony Worrall Thompson
ROSEMARY NEW POTATOES

I had to start these delicious potatoes in the microwave to ensure they cooked in time, but of course you could use leftover boiled new potatoes with excellent results. Serve them with succulent lamb or as a side order for a barbecue feast. ▶

Serves 2

225 g (8 oz) new potatoes
2 tbsp olive oil
2 garlic cloves, finely chopped
2 fresh rosemary sprigs
knob butter
Maldon sea salt and freshly ground
    black pepper

Slice the potatoes and place in a non-metallic bowl with a tablespoon of water. Cover with cling film and then pierce with a fork. Cook on high in the microwave for 3 minutes until almost tender.

Meanwhile, heat a non-stick frying pan. When the potatoes are ready, quickly drain off any excess water and dry on kitchen paper. Add the oil to the frying pan and then tip in the potatoes, garlic and rosemary, tossing to combine. Pan fry for 3–4 minutes until lightly golden – just be careful not to allow the garlic to burn.

Season the potatoes generously, add the butter, tossing to coat evenly, and then continue to sauté for another minute or two until the potatoes are completely tender and lightly golden. Pile into a warmed dish to serve, discarding any excess oil.

Antony Worrall Thompson
CAULIFLOWER CHEESE MASH

This is great served with ham or bacon, and if you fancy a change from the traditional cheese try using Dijon mustard, chopped capers and flat-leaf parsley instead. I would serve this variation with a gutsy game casserole.

Serves 2–4

1 small cauliflower, broken into
    small florets
25 g (1 oz) butter
1 small onion, finely chopped
100 g (4 oz) mature Cheddar,
    finely grated
85 ml (3 fl oz) double cream
pinch freshly grated nutmeg
salt and freshly ground white pepper

Cook the cauliflower florets for 6–8 minutes in a pan of boiling salted water until tender but not mushy.

Melt the butter in a large pan and gently pan-fry the onion for 4–5 minutes until well softened but not coloured. Transfer to a food processor and add the Cheddar and cream.

When the cauliflower is cooked, quickly drain and then either blend to a thick purée in the food processor or mash by hand with a potato masher. Season to taste and stir in the nutmeg. Transfer to a warmed bowl to serve.

Tony Tobin
GLAZED CARROTS

The sharp crunchiness of these carrots is a perfect foil for the creamy richness of the goat's cheese. Serve with a roast leg of spring lamb or some pan-fried hake or cod.

Serves 2

25 g (1 oz) butter
1 tbsp olive oil
275 g (10 oz) small carrots,
 cut on the diagonal
few whole coriander seeds
good pinch fresh thyme leaves
splash red wine vinegar
about 120 ml (4 fl oz) dry white wine
1 disc fresh soft goat's cheese
1 tsp chopped fresh flat-leaf parsley
salt and freshly ground black pepper

Heat half the butter and the olive oil in a pan. Add the carrots and sweat for a couple of minutes to soften without colouring.

Place the coriander seeds in a pestle and mortar and lightly crush, then tip into the pan with the thyme and vinegar, and season to taste. Pour in enough wine to barely cover the carrots and boil fast for 6–8 minutes until tender and all the liquid has evaporated.

Melt the remaining butter in a small frying pan and fry the goat's cheese disc for 1–2 minutes on each side until golden. Transfer the carrots to a warmed dish and scatter over the parsley. Arrange the goat's cheese disc on top to serve.

Brian Turner
CRUSHED NEW POTATOES WITH SPRING ONIONS

These potatoes are a kind of textured mash that you often see in trendy restaurants, so don't be tempted to make them too smooth. Pile them into a metal cooking ring set on the serving plate for a really professional result.

Serves 2

350 g (12 oz) tiny baby new potatoes,
 scraped or scrubbed
50 ml (2 fl oz) extra-virgin olive oil
2 spring onions, finely chopped
handful fresh basil leaves
salt and freshly ground black pepper

Place the potatoes in a large pan of boiling water and bring to the boil. Cover and simmer for about 8 minutes until tender, then drain well.

Warm the olive oil in a small pan with the spring onions until the spring onions have softened but not coloured.

Tip the cooked potatoes into a large bowl. Add the warmed olive oil and spring onion mixture and, with the back of a fork, gently crush each potato until it just splits. Season, and then mix carefully until all the oil has been absorbed. Finely chop the basil and stir through the potatoes. Season to taste and pile into a bowl to serve.

Gino D'Acampo
CREAMED SWEET POTATOES

I prefer to use the orange-fleshed sweet potatoes as their colour is so much more dramatic. However, the yellow-coloured variety tastes just as good.

Serves 2

350 g (12 oz) sweet potatoes, peeled and cut into small cubes (orange-fleshed if possible)
25 g (1 oz) butter
4 tbsp double cream
1 tbsp chopped fresh flat-leaf parsley
salt and freshly ground black pepper

Place the sweet potatoes in a pan of boiling water, cover and cook for 8 minutes until cooked through and tender.

Drain the sweet potatoes and blitz with a hand blender until smooth. Add the butter, cream and parsley, and season to taste. Blitz again briefly to combine.

Spoon the creamed sweet potatoes into a warmed dish and serve at once.

Paul Rankin
EGG-FRIED RICE

Whenever I cook rice, I always make more than I need so that I have leftovers to use for dishes like this. To prevent leftover rice from sticking together in one solid mass, stir in a little sunflower oil before refrigerating it.

Serves 2

2 tsp sunflower oil
250 g (9 oz) packet cooked white rice (or use leftover rice)
4 spring onions, finely chopped
1 mild green chilli, seeded and finely chopped
1 tbsp chopped fresh coriander
1 egg, beaten
1 tsp snipped fresh chives
salt and freshly ground black pepper
dark soy sauce, to serve

Heat a wok until very hot. Add the oil, swirling it up the sides, then tip the rice into the wok and stir-fry for 2–3 minutes until piping hot. Add the spring onions, chilli and coriander, then season to taste, tossing to combine all the ingredients.

Make a small well in the middle of the rice, quickly pour in the beaten egg, then continue to stir for 30 seconds until the egg is lightly scrambled. Finally fold into the rice and divide among warmed bowls or plates. Garnish with the chives and serve at once, with dark soy sauce to hand around.

on the side

73

Nick Nairn
GRIDDLED POLENTA WITH ROAST PEPPER AND BASIL DRESSING

As with all simple dishes the quality of ingredients is of paramount importance, so try to get Italian ready-made polenta – it's by far the best. Look out for jars of wood-roasted peppers, too; both should be available in good delicatessens. I like to serve this with a char-grilled chicken fillet or piece of fish. ◄

Serves 2

225 g (8 oz) roll ready-made polenta
1 tbsp olive oil
1 roasted red pepper, drained
    (from a jar)
2 tbsp extra-virgin olive oil
finely grated rind of 1 lemon
small handful fresh basil leaves,
    shredded
1 garlic clove, crushed
salt and freshly ground black pepper

Heat a large griddle pan until very hot. Cut the polenta into 1 cm (½ in) slices – you'll need about six in total. Brush on both sides with the olive oil and arrange on the heated griddle pan. Cook for 2–3 minutes on each side until nicely marked and heated through.

Meanwhile, make the roast pepper and basil dressing. Cut the pepper into strips, discarding any seeds, then finely dice. Place in a bowl with the extra-virgin olive oil, lemon rind, basil and garlic. Season to taste and stir until well combined.

Divide the griddled polenta between warmed plates and spoon over the dressing to serve.

Phil Vickery
RICOTTA AND SPINACH-STUFFED TOMATOES

If time allowed, I'd sprinkle the insides of the scooped-out tomatoes with a little salt, then turn them upside down and set them aside on kitchen paper to allow the excess juices to drain away. Serve these with some pan-fried fish or chicken.

Serves 2

1 tsp olive oil, plus extra for greasing
100 g (4 oz) baby spinach leaves
150 g (5 oz) ricotta cheese
squeeze lemon juice
pinch freshly grated nutmeg
2 ripe tomatoes
salt and freshly ground black pepper

Preheat the oven to 220°C/425°F/Gas 7. Heat the oil in a pan and tip in the spinach. Season to taste and cook for 1 minute until wilted, stirring continuously. Drain off any excess moisture and place in a bowl.

Add the ricotta to the wilted spinach with the lemon juice and nutmeg. Season to taste and mix until combined.

Slice the top off each tomato and discard, then, being careful not to damage the skin, scoop out the seeds. Place in a lightly oiled baking dish and divide the ricotta and spinach mixture between them.

Roast the stuffed tomatoes for 6–8 minutes until the tomatoes have slightly softened but are still holding their shape and the filling has heated through. Serve at once.

on the side

75

James Martin
LEMON COUSCOUS

Perfect as an accompaniment to fish or as part of a barbecue spread. It's great hot or cold and can be made 24 hours in advance. ▶

Serves 2

120 ml (4 fl oz) hot chicken stock
100 g (4 oz) couscous
finely grated rind and juice ½ lemon
2 tbsp extra-virgin olive oil
1 baby yellow pepper
1 baby fennel
1 shallot
2 tbsp chopped mixed fresh flat-leaf
   parsley and coriander
salt and freshly ground black pepper
lemon wedges, to garnish

Heat the stock in a small pan until boiling. Place the couscous in a large heatproof bowl with the lemon juice and olive oil, stirring to combine. Pour over the stock, then stir well, cover and leave to stand for 5 minutes.

Meanwhile, cut the yellow pepper in half, remove the seeds and finely dice. Finely dice the baby fennel and the shallot and set aside until needed.

Separate the couscous grains with a fork. Season to taste and place in a pan to reheat, stirring continuously with a fork. Remove from the heat and fold in the lemon rind, herbs, pepper, fennel and shallot, then season to taste. Spoon onto a platter and garnish with lemon wedges to serve.

❝ We're capable of shallot ❞

Ross Burden
BLACK BEAN SALSA

This salsa is almost a salad in its own right, particularly if you were to add some cooked sweetcorn or podded broad beans. Try it with char-grilled pork or lamb chops, or with a bowl of tortilla chips as part of a Mexican feast.

Serves 2–4

1 roasted red pepper, drained
   (from a jar)
400 g (14 oz) can black beans,
   drained and rinsed
½ small red onion, finely chopped
2 tbsp chopped fresh flat-leaf parsley
pinch dried crushed chillies
1 tbsp extra-virgin olive oil
2 tsp freshly squeezed lemon juice
salt and freshly ground black pepper

Cut the roasted red pepper in half and remove any remaining seeds, then finely dice the flesh and place in a bowl.

Add the black beans to the bowl with the red onion, parsley, crushed chillies, olive oil and lemon juice. Season to taste and leave the flavours to combine for as long as time allows. To serve, use as required.

Lesley Waters
STIR-FRIED PAK CHOI WITH CHILLI

Any leafy green vegetable that has a bit of crunch will work well cooked in this manner, so experiment with curly kale, Chinese cabbage, spring greens or even Brussels sprout tops.

Serves 2

2 tsp sunflower oil
3 spring onions, finely chopped
1 garlic clove, crushed
1 tsp freshly grated root ginger
1 mild red chilli, seeded and very thinly sliced
2 pak choi, shredded (about 200 g (7 oz) in total)
dash dark soy sauce
1 tsp sesame seeds

Heat a wok until very hot. Add the oil, swirling up the sides, and then add the spring onions, garlic, ginger and chilli. Stir-fry for 1 minute until softened but not coloured.

Add the pak choi to the wok and stir-fry for another minute, then sprinkle over two tablespoons of water. Reduce the heat and steam-fry for another 2–3 minutes until tender.

Sprinkle over the soy sauce and sesame seeds, then toss until just combined. Tip onto a warmed platter and serve at once.

Ross Burden
PINEAPPLE RELISH

A relish to accompany curries or spicy barbecue dishes. It would be especially good with chicken fajitas or chicken fried in a spiced breadcrumb coating. It should last for up to one week in the fridge.

Serves 2–4

1 miniature pineapple
1 mild red chilli, seeded and finely chopped
1 tbsp chopped fresh coriander
juice 1 lime
2 tbsp olive oil
salt and freshly ground black pepper

To prepare the pineapple, cut off the leaf crown and bottom so that it sits flat. Using a sharp knife, remove the skin by cutting down the length of the fruit. Cut the flesh into quarters lengthways and remove the woody core. Finely dice the remaining flesh and place in a bowl.

Add the chilli to the pineapple with the coriander, lime juice and oil. Season to taste and mix well to combine. Leave to stand at room temperature until ready to serve, to allow the flavours to develop.

James Tanner
PAD THAI

I could never tire of Pad Thai – to me it is one of the world's great dishes. This is a version I made up using the ingredients I had to hand, but the basic principles are still the same.

Serves 2

100 g (4 oz) soba noodles
2 tsp sesame seeds
2 tbsp sunflower oil
4 spring onions, finely chopped
2 garlic cloves, finely chopped
2.5 cm (1 in) piece root ginger, peeled and finely chopped
2 tbsp dark soy sauce
juice ½ lime
1 baby pak choi, shredded
1 egg, beaten

Bring a large pan of water to the boil. Add the soba noodles, stir until it comes to a second boil and continue boiling for 4 minutes or until tender but firm to the bite. Drain in a colander. Rinse thoroughly with boiling water and drain again.

Meanwhile, heat a wok until very hot. Toast the sesame seeds in a dry frying pan, tossing occasionally to ensure that they cook evenly. Tip onto a plate and leave to cool.

When the noodles are ready, add the oil to the heated wok and swirl up the sides, then add the spring onions, garlic and ginger and stir-fry for 20 seconds. Tip in the drained soba noodles and drizzle over soy sauce and lime juice, then stir-fry for 1–2 minutes until heated through

Add the pak choi to the noodle mixture and continue to stir-fry for a minute or so until wilted. Make a small well in the middle of the noodle mixture, quickly pour in the beaten egg, then continue to stir for 1 minute until the egg is lightly scrambled. Fold into the noodles and spoon into a warmed dish to serve.

❝It's all a bit oriental!❞

on the side

vegetarian

Nick Nairn
SPINACH RAVIOLI WITH PARMESAN CREAM

This quick and easy dish is made using the wonton wrappers available from Chinese supermarkets and other Asian stores. They freeze brilliantly, so the rest of the packet can be used at a later stage, and although they are very thin, they are much sturdier than traditional homemade pasta and therefore much easier to use.

Serves 2

100 g (4 oz) tender young spinach
   leaves
small knob butter
50 g (2 oz) ricotta cheese
25 g (1 oz) freshly grated Parmesan
1 small garlic clove, crushed
pinch freshly grated nutmeg
24 wonton wrappers, thawed if frozen
1 egg yolk, lightly beaten

FOR THE PARMESAN CREAM
120 ml (4 fl oz) double cream
50 g (2 oz) freshly grated Parmesan
salt and freshly ground black pepper

Bring a large pan of salted water to a rolling boil. Place the spinach in a small pan with the butter and season generously, then cook until just wilted. Tip into a sieve and drain well of excess moisture, then roughly chop and place in a bowl.

Mix the ricotta into the spinach with the Parmesan, garlic and nutmeg. Take a wonton wrapper and brush the edges with a little of the egg yolk. Place a spoonful of the spinach mixture in the middle and then place another wonton wrapper on top, pressing down the edges to seal. Repeat until you have 12 ravioli in total.

To make the Parmesan cream, place the cream in a small pan and cook for a few minutes until slightly reduced and thickened, then stir in the Parmesan until melted. Remove from the heat and keep warm.

Meanwhile, gently lower the ravioli into the pan of boiling salted water and simmer for 1–2 minutes until they are cooked through and floating on the top. Lift out with a slotted spoon, gently shaking off any excess water and arrange in warmed serving plates. Ladle over the Parmesan cream and serve at once.

'You ricotta agree, this'll leave you wonton more'

vegetarian

81

Tony Tobin
STUFFED FIELD MUSHROOMS

Flat (field) mushrooms are full of flavour and perfect for roasting. It's important not to wash them – just wipe them with a damp cloth or gently brush off any dirt. ▸

Serves 2

6 large flat mushrooms, stalks removed (each about 7.5 cm/3 in in diameter)
olive oil, for drizzling
25 g (1 oz) butter
2 garlic cloves, crushed
2 tbsp chopped fresh mixed herbs (such as flat-leaf parsley, basil and chives)
50 g (2 oz) fresh white breadcrumbs
6 small discs fresh goat's cheese
50 g (2 oz) wild rocket
a little extra-virgin olive oil
dash balsamic vinegar
salt and freshly ground black pepper

Preheat the oven to 220°C/425°F/Gas 7 and place the mushrooms in a non-stick baking tin. Season lightly and drizzle a little olive oil over each one. Bake in the oven for 3–4 minutes.

Meanwhile, melt the butter in a frying pan over a low heat. Sauté the garlic, herbs, breadcrumbs and seasoning for a few minutes until lightly golden.

Take the mushrooms from the oven and divide the breadcrumbs between them. Place a disc of goat's cheese on each and return to the oven for 5 minutes, until the breadcrumbs are golden and the cheese has melted.

Place the rocket leaves in a bowl and barely coat them with extra-virgin olive oil and balsamic vinegar. Season to taste. Arrange the mushrooms on plates and serve the rocket salad to the side.

Brian Turner
WILD MUSHROOM OMELETTE

Omelettes are so quick to make that it's just not worth cooking a large one for two. Don't be tempted to over-beat the eggs – that will spoil the texture.

Serves 1

2 tsp sunflower oil
knob butter
100 g (4 oz) mixed wild mushrooms, sliced
4 tbsp double cream
3 eggs
1 tbsp chopped mixed fresh herbs (such as flat-leaf parsley, chives and basil)
salt and freshly ground black pepper
crusty French bread, to serve

Preheat the grill and heat a non-stick frying pan with a base about 20 cm (8 in) in diameter. Place half of the oil and butter in a separate frying pan and once the butter is foaming, tip in the wild mushrooms. Season to taste and then sauté for 2–3 minutes until tender. Stir in the cream and cook gently for another minute or two.

Meanwhile, break the eggs into a bowl and add the herbs, then season and lightly beat. When the non-stick frying pan is hot, add the remaining oil and butter, swirling it round the base and sides.

While the butter is still foaming, pour in the eggs, tilting the pan from side to side. Stir gently with a fork or wooden spatula, drawing the mixture from the sides to the centre as it sets. When almost set, carefully turn the omelette and cook for another minute. Tilt the pan away from you slightly and use a palette knife to fold over a third of the omelette to the centre, then fold over the opposite third. Slide onto a warmed plate, allowing it to flip over so the fold is underneath. Spoon over the wild mushroom cream and eat at once with crusty French bread.

Phil Vickery
SPINACH AND GOAT'S CHEESE ROULADE

To make this dish in less than ten you've got to work very quickly for the first couple of minutes. The results are worth it and look spectacular.

Serves 2

knob butter, plus extra for greasing
100 g (4 oz) tender young spinach
    leaves
4 eggs, separated
2 tbsp plain flour
pinch English mustard powder
1 tbsp snipped fresh chives
1 tbsp chopped fresh chervil
50 g (2 oz) soft goat's cheese,
    finely diced

FOR THE TOMATO SALAD

3 ripe plum tomatoes
2 spring onions, finely chopped
1 tbsp shredded fresh basil
dash balsamic vinegar
good glug extra-virgin olive oil
salt and freshly ground black pepper

Preheat the oven to 240°C/475°F/Gas 9. Grease and line a Swiss roll tin with non-stick parchment paper. Heat the butter in a pan and tip in the spinach. Cook for a minute or so until wilted, stirring occasionally. Season to taste, then drain off excess moisture.

Meanwhile, whisk the egg whites in a large bowl until soft peaks have formed. Sieve in the flour and continue to whisk until stiff peaks have formed.

Place the egg yolks in a separate bowl and stir in the mustard powder, then fold into the egg white mixture until just combined. Transfer to the lined Swiss roll tin and smooth over with a spatula.

Sprinkle the herbs over the roulade mixture and then scatter the wilted spinach and goat's cheese on top. Bake for about 8 minutes until cooked through and lightly golden.

To make the tomato salad, cut the tomatoes into wedges and place in a bowl with the spring onions, basil, vinegar and olive oil. Season to taste and mix gently to combine.

Remove the roulade from the oven and, using a tea towel to protect your fingers, quickly roll up. Cut the roulade into slices and serve on plates with some of the tomato salad.

Lesley Waters
TAGLIATELLE WITH MUSHROOMS AND HERB PESTO

A word of warning: don't dredge the pasta in flour to prevent it from sticking in the pasta machine, as the flour turns glue-like when cooked and, ironically, causes the pasta to stick together.

Serves 2

knob butter
2 flat mushrooms, chopped
1 garlic clove, crushed
50 ml (2 fl oz) dry white wine
85 ml (3 fl oz) double cream
bunch mixed fresh soft herbs (such as basil, flat-leaf parsley and chives)
1 garlic clove, chopped
2 tbsp toasted chopped walnuts
4 tbsp extra-virgin olive oil

FOR THE PASTA DOUGH
150 g (5 oz) Italian '00' flour
1 egg
1 egg yolk
dash olive oil
salt and freshly ground black pepper

Bring a large pan of salted water to the boil. To make the dough, place the flour in a food processor with the egg, egg yolk, olive oil and a pinch of salt. Blend until the ingredients come together and resemble a dough.

Turn out onto a floured board and knead for 2 minutes until smooth and pliable. Roll out with a rolling pin and cut into two pieces, then pass through the widest setting of a pasta machine. Repeat this process, decreasing the roller setting down grade by grade with each pass, taking it down to the second-lowest setting. Finally pass through the cutting rollers to make tagliatelle. Repeat with the remaining piece of dough.

Meanwhile, heat a large frying pan. Add the butter and sauté the mushrooms and garlic for 3–4 minutes until tender and all the liquid has evaporated. Season to taste. Pour in the wine and allow to bubble right down, then stir in the cream and cook for a minute or so until slightly reduced.

Plunge the tagliatelle into the pan of boiling water and stir once, then cook for 2 minutes until tender.

To make the herb pesto, strip the herb leaves from the stalks and place in a mini food processor with the garlic, walnuts and olive oil. Blend until smooth. Season to taste.

Drain the pasta and then tip into the mushroom sauce, tossing to coat. Divide between warmed wide-rimmed bowls and drizzle over the herb pesto to serve.

‘ Hey pesto ,

vegetarian

85

Phil Vickery
AUBERGINE AND MOZZARELLA WRAPS WITH ROCKET DRESSING

Char-grilled aubergine antipasto is now available in most major supermarkets; each jar should have at least four slices in it. Or you can always cook slices of aubergine brushed with olive oil on the griddle pan, then simply continue with the recipe as described below. ◄

Serves 2

1 small ripe plum tomato
150 g (5 oz) ball buffalo
   mozzarella, drained
300 g (11 oz) jar char-grilled aubergine
   antipasto, drained
handful fresh basil leaves
4 sun-dried tomatoes in oil, drained
   and finely chopped

FOR THE ROCKET DRESSING
1 tsp white wine vinegar
squeeze lemon juice
3 tbsp extra-virgin olive oil
25 g (1 oz) wild rocket
salt and freshly ground black pepper

Heat a griddle pan until very hot. Cut the tomato into four thick slices, discarding the ends. Cut the mozzarella ball into four even slices. Place the char-grilled aubergine slices on the work surface and place a piece of tomato in the middle of each slice. Arrange the mozzarella slices on top. Roughly tear the basil and scatter on top with the sun-dried tomatoes. Season with plenty of pepper.

Flip over both ends of each piece of aubergine to enclose the filling and secure with wooden cocktail sticks. Place the wraps on the heated griddle pan and cook for 1–2 minutes on each side until heated through and lightly golden.

Make the rocket dressing. Place the vinegar, lemon juice, olive oil and rocket in a mini food processor and blend until smooth. Season to taste. Arrange the wraps on warmed plates and drizzle over the dressing to serve.

Paul Rankin
CHICKPEA AND POTATO CURRY

I'm always rustling up curries like this at home – a reminder of our travels in southern India.

Serves 2

2 tbsp sunflower oil
1 onion, thinly sliced
2 mild green chillies, seeded and
   finely chopped
2 tbsp hot curry paste (such as Madras)
100 ml (3½ fl oz) hot vegetable stock
   (from a cube is fine)
200 g (7 oz) can chickpeas, rinsed and
   drained
225 g (8 oz) cooked baby potatoes,
   peeled and quartered
1 tbsp Greek yoghurt
2 naan breads
salt and freshly ground black pepper
chopped fresh coriander, to garnish

Preheat the grill. Heat the oil in a pan and fry the onion and chillies for a few minutes until softened and just beginning to colour, stirring occasionally. Add the curry paste and cook for another minute or so, stirring. Pour in the stock, stir and bring to a simmer. Season to taste.

Add the chickpeas and potatoes to the pan and simmer for a few minutes until heated through, stirring occasionally. Stir in the yoghurt and just warm through.

Meanwhile, sprinkle the naan breads with a little water and arrange on the grill rack. Cook for a few minutes until heated through or according to packet instructions.

Arrange the naan breads on warmed plates and spoon the chickpea and potato curry on top. Scatter over the coriander to garnish and serve at once.

vegetarian

James Tanner
OMELETTE-WRAPPED STIR-FRIED AUBERGINE WITH TOFU

I was very pleased with this dish on the programme. I think it would make a fantastic mid-week supper. I really like the soft, silky texture of the chilli-flavoured aubergine and it combined very well with the tofu, which can otherwise be a bit boring.

Serves 2

about 2 tbsp sunflower oil
1 tbsp sesame oil, plus a little extra
2 garlic cloves, finely chopped
1 mild red chilli, seeded and finely chopped
1 small aubergine, cut into 1 cm (½ in) cubes
3 eggs
50 ml (2 fl oz) coconut milk
1 tbsp dark soy sauce, plus a little extra
2 tbsp sesame seeds
juice 1 lime
100 g (4 oz) firm white tofu, cut into 1 cm (½ in) cubes
fresh coriander sprigs, to garnish

Heat a wok until very hot. Add one tablespoon of the sunflower oil and the sesame oil and swirl up the sides of the pan. Tip in the garlic, chilli and aubergine and stir-fry for 5 minutes until the aubergine is tender.

Meanwhile, heat a non-stick frying pan whose base is about 20 cm (8 in) in diameter. Crack the eggs into a bowl and add the coconut milk with a dash of soy sauce and sesame oil. Lightly beat with a fork. Add a thin film of sunflower oil to the frying pan and then pour in half of the egg mixture, swirling it around so it fills the pan. Cook for a minute or two until golden brown underneath but still slightly soft on top. Slide out onto a flat plate and keep warm.

Meanwhile, sprinkle the sesame seeds into the wok, tossing to combine, then drizzle over the tablespoon of soy sauce and the lime juice. Scatter over the tofu, again tossing to combine, and continue to cook for a minute or so until the tofu is heated through.

Meanwhile, make a second omelette in the same way as the first and pile half of the aubergine and tofu mixture in the centre. Fold in the edges like a parcel and then flip onto a warmed plate. Repeat until you have two omelette parcels, then garnish with the coriander sprigs and serve at once.

James Martin
CHEESY POLENTA WITH WILTED SPINACH AND ROASTED SHALLOTS

This is a satisfying vegetarian main course. It was a great success when I made it on the programme.

Serves 2

2 tbsp olive oil, plus a little extra
5 small shallots, peeled and halved
pinch caster sugar
good pinch fresh soft thyme leaves
225 g (8 oz) tender young spinach leaves
pinch freshly grated nutmeg
200 g (7 oz) instant polenta
1 garlic clove, crushed
100 g (4 oz) cambozola cheese, rind removed, finely diced
salt and freshly ground black pepper

Preheat the oven to 200°C/400°F/Gas 6. Heat an ovenproof frying pan and add the two tablespoons of olive oil. Sauté the shallots for a couple of minutes until lightly golden. Sprinkle with the sugar and thyme, then season to taste, tossing to coat evenly. Transfer to the oven for another 5 minutes or so until cooked through and tender.

Heat 600 ml (1 pint) of water until boiling.

Place a dash of the olive oil in a pan and add the spinach. Season to taste and add a little nutmeg, then stir until just wilted. Drain off any excess moisture and keep warm.

When the water is boiling, add a good pinch of salt and then slowly pour in the polenta in a thin, continuous stream. Add the garlic and continue to stir until the polenta begins to thicken – this should take about 1 minute. Stir in the cambozola until melted and season to taste.

Divide the cheesy polenta between warmed plates and arrange the spinach and roasted shallots on top to serve.

' Polenta dishes for you to admire '

Gino D'Acampo
CHILLI BROCCOLI AND MANGO NOODLE STIR-FRY

To make this more substantial, whisk two eggs with a dash of soy and swirl up the sides of a heated wok with a tablespoon of oil in it. Roll up like a pancake and shred before adding back into the noodle mixture to just warm through. ▸

Serves 2

100 g (4 oz) medium egg noodles
2 tbsp sunflower oil
225 g (8 oz) long-stemmed broccoli florets, trimmed
4 spring onions, finely chopped
1 small green mango, peeled and cut into slices
1 red scotch bonnet chilli, seeded and thinly sliced
1 tbsp chopped fresh coriander
few drops sesame oil
salt and freshly ground black pepper

Drop the noodles into a pan of boiling water and remove from the heat. Stir with a fork and then leave to stand for 4 minutes or according to packet instructions until tender. Stir again and drain well.

Heat a wok or large frying pan until very hot. Add the oil to the wok, swirling it up the sides, then add the broccoli. Stir-fry for 3–4 minutes until just beginning to soften.

Add the spring onions to the broccoli and stir-fry for another minute or two. Using a wooden spatula, fold in the mango slices with the drained noodles.

Add the chilli to the wok, season to taste and continue to stir-fry for another 1–2 minutes until the broccoli is completely tender and cooked through. Fold in the coriander and sprinkle with the sesame oil. Divide between warmed bowls to serve.

James Tanner
LEMON, ROCKET AND TALEGGIO PASTA

Taleggio is a readily available, creamy, semi-soft Italian rinded cheese. Be careful not to overcook it or it can become stringy and rubbery.

Serves 2

225 g (8 oz) fresh fettuccine pasta (good quality)
4 tbsp dry white wine
2 garlic cloves, finely chopped
finely grated rind of 1 lemon
4 tbsp double cream
40 g (1½ oz) rocket leaves
100 g (4 oz) taleggio cheese, rind removed, cut into cubes
salt and freshly ground black pepper

Plunge the fettuccine into a large pan of boiling salted water and cook for 2–3 minutes or according to packet instructions. Drain and quickly refresh under cold running water.

Place the wine in a large wide pan with the garlic and lemon rind and cook over a gentle heat for 2–3 minutes to allow the flavours to infuse and the liquid to slightly reduce. Add the cream and season to taste. Cut the lemon in half and add a squeeze of the juice.

Fold in the cooked fettuccine with the rocket and taleggio and keep over a low heat until the cheese has begun to melt. Divide between warmed wide-rimmed bowls and serve at once.

Antony Worrall Thompson

THAI VEGETABLE AND NOODLE COCONUT STIR-FRY

This recipe is based on how I normally make my Thai chicken curry, full of lovely tastes and textures with plenty of crunchy vegetables. But be warned, it's moreish. Don't be surprised if everyone comes back for second helpings...

Serves 2

1 garlic clove, roughly chopped

1 lemon grass stalk, trimmed and roughly chopped

small bunch fresh coriander (roots intact if possible)

small handful fresh mint leaves

pinch dried crushed chillies

1 tbsp sunflower oil

250 ml (8½ fl oz) carton coconut cream

2 small carrots, thinly sliced on the diagonal

1 small red pepper, halved, seeded and thinly sliced

75 g (3 oz) small broccoli florets

50 g (2 oz) chestnut mushrooms, sliced

100 g (4 oz) packet express cooked egg noodles

4 spring onions, shredded

Heat a large pan or wok. Place the garlic in a mini food processor with the lemon grass, coriander, mint, crushed chillies and oil. Blitz to a fine paste. Add to the heated wok and stir-fry for 1–2 minutes until fragrant.

Pour the coconut cream into the pan and bring to a simmer, then add the carrots, red pepper, broccoli florets and mushrooms. Cook for 4–5 minutes until all the vegetables are tender, stirring occasionally.

Add the noodles to the pan with the spring onions and toss until well combined, then continue to cook for another 1–2 minutes until completely heated through. Divide between warmed plates and serve at once.

'Thai flies when you're having fun'

Ross Burden
GNOCCHI WITH BASIL PESTO

Freshly made gnocchi tastes so much better than bought and it's far easier than you might imagine. Experiment with the sauce you serve it with. Try a walnut and flat-leaf parsley pesto or a simple tomato sauce for a change.

Serves 2

75 g (3 oz) frozen leaf spinach
75 g (3 oz) freshly grated Parmesan,
    plus extra to serve
125 g (4½ oz) ricotta cheese
50 g (2 oz) type '00' pasta flour,
    plus extra for dusting
1 egg
pinch freshly grated nutmeg

FOR THE BASIL PESTO

25 g (1 oz) pine nuts
good handful fresh basil leaves
25 g (1 oz) freshly grated Parmesan
about 6 tbsp extra-virgin olive oil
salt and freshly ground black pepper

To make the basil pesto, place the pine nuts in a dry frying pan and cook for about 5 minutes until lightly golden and toasted, tossing occasionally to ensure they cook evenly. Tip out onto a tray and leave to cool completely.

Meanwhile, to make the gnocchi, bring a large pan of salted water to the boil. Thaw the spinach in the microwave and then place in a clean tea towel and squeeze out the excess moisture. Finely chop and place in a large bowl with the Parmesan, ricotta, flour and egg. Season to taste and add the nutmeg, then mix until well combined, using your hands.

Bring the spinach mixture together as a dough and place on a lightly floured board. Using floured hands, roll into a long sausage shape that is no more than 1 cm (½ in) thick, then cut off 2 cm (¾ in) pieces.

Drop the gnocchi into the boiling salted water and cook for 3–4 minutes or until they have risen to the surface.

Meanwhile, finish making the basil pesto. Place the cooled toasted pine nuts in a mini food processor with the basil and Parmesan. Slowly add enough of the olive oil through the feeder tube to form a smooth emulsion. Season to taste.

Drain the gnocchi and return to the pan. Add the pesto and toss until well combined. Divide among warmed wide-rimmed bowls and garnish with extra Parmesan to serve.

vegetarian

seafood

Paul Rankin
CRISPY HADDOCK WITH SWEET AND SOUR SAUCE

There's nothing quite like crispy haddock in batter. The technique I've used for the batter would work well with any firm-fleshed fish, such as cod, sole or salmon.

Serves 2

sunflower oil, for deep-frying
275 g (10 oz) haddock fillet, skinned
   and any bones removed
1 egg white
120 ml (4 fl oz) double cream
4 tbsp plain flour
handful baby spinach leaves

FOR THE SWEET AND SOUR SAUCE
2 tbsp olive oil
1 small red pepper, halved, seeded
   and finely diced
1 garlic clove, crushed
pinch dried crushed chillies
1 tsp red wine vinegar
1 tbsp caster sugar
1 tbsp tomato ketchup
salt and freshly ground black pepper

Heat a deep fat fryer to 190°C/375°F or fill a deep-sided pan one-third full with sunflower oil. If you don't have a thermometer, the oil should be hot enough so that when a bread cube is added, it browns in 40 seconds.

Meanwhile, make the sweet and sour sauce. Heat the olive oil in a frying pan and sauté the red pepper for 3–4 minutes until tender but not coloured. Stir in the garlic and then add the crushed chillies, vinegar, sugar and tomato ketchup, and simmer for 4–5 minutes until well reduced and thickened. Add one to two tablespoons of water to the sauce if you think it needs it, and season to taste.

Meanwhile, cut the haddock on the diagonal into 5 cm (2 in) strips. Lightly beat the egg white and cream together in a shallow dish. Tip the flour onto a flat plate and season generously.

Coat the haddock strips in the seasoned flour, shaking off any excess and then dip into the egg mixture. Quickly coat again in the flour and drop into the hot oil. Deep-fry the haddock for 2–3 minutes until cooked through and golden brown. Drain on kitchen paper.

Divide the spinach between warmed plates and arrange the crispy haddock on top. Drizzle over the sweet and sour sauce to serve.

'Causing haddock in the kitchen'

seafood

James Tanner
STIR-FRIED PRAWNS WITH PAK CHOI AND CHILLI GLAZE

This is a fantastic way to cook tiger prawns – the chilli glaze gives them a wonderful coating and the pak choi provides much-needed crunch. Serve with bowls of steaming Thai fragrant rice. ◀

Serves 2

1 tbsp white wine vinegar
2 garlic cloves, crushed
2 cm (¾ in) piece root ginger, peeled and finely grated
1 tsp caster sugar
1 mild red chilli, seeded and finely chopped
1 tbsp sunflower oil
4 spring onions, finely chopped
275 g (10 oz) raw peeled tiger prawns
1 pak choi, cut on the diagonal into 2.5 cm (1 in) strips
small handful torn fresh coriander leaves

Place the vinegar, garlic, ginger and sugar in a small pan with half of the chilli. Bring to the boil, reduce the heat and simmer for 4–5 minutes until well reduced and slightly sticky.

Meanwhile, heat a wok until very hot. Add the sunflower oil and swirl up around the sides, then tip in the remaining chilli with the spring onions and stir-fry for 20 seconds. Add the prawns and pak choi and continue to stir-fry for 2–3 minutes until tender, tossing regularly.

Drizzle the chilli glaze into the wok, tossing to combine, and then scatter over the coriander leaves. When everything is nicely glazed, divide between warmed plates and serve at once.

James Martin
BUTTERFLIED SARDINES WITH ORANGE AND FENNEL SALAD

Spanking-fresh sardines are superb, not a bit like tinned ones. Ask your fishmonger to gut and scale the fish, and to remove the heads if you're put off by gleaming eyes staring at you.

Serves 2

4 fresh sardines, cleaned
2 tbsp olive oil, plus a little extra
2 oranges
2 baby fennel
1 tbsp chopped fresh dill
salt and freshly ground black pepper

Preheat the grill to high. Remove the heads from the sardines, if necessary, and split them down the middle on the underside. Press down along the backbone, turn over and then carefully remove the backbone, cutting off the bone just before the tail. Arrange the butterflied sardines on a grill rack and season to taste, then drizzle with a little olive oil and cook for 3–4 minutes until just tender, turning once.

Meanwhile, make the salad. Cut the skin from one of the oranges and remove all the white pith. Carefully cut into segments over a bowl to catch any juices. Cut the other orange in half and squeeze the juice on top. Cut the fennel into wafer-thin slices on a mandolin and add to the orange mixture with the two tablespoons of olive oil and dill. Season to taste and toss until well combined.

Divide the orange and fennel salad between two plates and arrange the butterflied sardines on top to serve.

James Tanner
SEARED TUNA WITH SWEET POTATO CRISPS AND PEACH SALSA

Tuna steaks can vary in thickness, so judging how long they need to cook might be difficult. The way to do it is to keep an eye on the side of the steaks, and when they look cooked a quarter of the way up, turn them over.

Serves 2

sunflower oil, for deep-frying
1 tsp olive oil
2 x 100 g (4 oz) fresh tuna steaks, each about 2.5 cm (1 in) thick
1 orange-fleshed sweet potato (no more than 225 g (8 oz) in total)
1 tbsp medium curry powder

FOR THE PEACH SALSA
1 tbsp olive oil
1 tbsp balsamic vinegar
1 ripe peach, halved, stoned and diced
10 cherry tomatoes, quartered
2 tbsp shredded fresh basil
salt and freshly ground black pepper

Preheat a deep-fat fryer or fill a deep-sided pan one-third full with oil and heat to 190°C/375°F. If you don't have a thermometer, the oil should be hot enough so that when a bread cube is added, it browns in 40 seconds.

Heat a griddle pan until very hot. Meanwhile, make the peach salsa. Heat the olive oil and balsamic vinegar in a small pan for 2–3 minutes. Place the peach in a bowl with the cherry tomatoes and basil. Season to taste and then fold in the hot olive oil and balsamic mixture. Set aside to allow the flavours to develop.

Drizzle the heated griddle pan with the olive oil and cook the tuna steaks for 2–3 minutes on each side, depending on how rare you like your fish.

Using a mandolin, cut the sweet potato into wafer-thin slices and deep-fry in batches for 30 seconds to 1 minute until crisp and lightly golden. Mix the curry powder in a small bowl with a tablespoon of salt. Tip the deep-fried sweet potato crisps onto kitchen paper and quickly and liberally dust with the curried salt.

Arrange the seared tuna on warmed plates and pile up a stack of the sweet potato crisps to the side. Add a generous dollop of the peach salsa and serve at once.

Antony Worrall Thompson
TUNA TORTILLA WITH GUACAMOLE

Soft flour tortilla wraps are a healthy and tasty alternative to traditional breads. For a packed lunch, simply spread the tuna mixture all over the tortillas and roll them up.

Serves 2

200 g (7 oz) can tuna in olive oil,
   drained
400 g (14 oz) can cannellini beans,
   drained and rinsed
2 ripe tomatoes, halved, seeded
   and diced
2 spring onions, finely chopped
1 tbsp extra-virgin olive oil
4 tbsp Greek yoghurt
2 soft flour tortillas

FOR THE GUACAMOLE

1 small ripe avocado
1 tomato, halved, seeded and diced
2 spring onions, finely chopped
1 garlic clove, crushed
2 tbsp chopped fresh coriander
pinch ground cumin
pinch ground coriander
juice 1 lime
2 tbsp extra-virgin olive oil
salt and freshly ground
   black pepper

Preheat the oven to 220°C/425°F/Gas 7. Place the tuna in a bowl with the cannellini beans, tomato, spring onions, oil and yoghurt. Season generously and mix well to combine.

Divide the tuna mixture between the two tortillas, spooning it into the centre. Fold over the edges to form a neat parcel, then pin in place with wooden cocktail sticks. Arrange the two parcels on a baking sheet and bake for 4–5 minutes until heated through.

Meanwhile, make the guacamole. Cut the avocado in half and remove the stone, then scoop out the flesh into a bowl, reserving the shells. Roughly mash with a fork, then add the tomato, spring onions, garlic, coriander, spices, lime juice and olive oil. Season to taste and mix well to combine. Spoon back into the avocado shells and arrange on plates with the hot tuna tortillas that have been cut on the diagonal to serve.

❝ All wrapped up and no place to go ❞

seafood

99

Brian Turner
HADDOCK MONTE CARLO

This dish worked a treat – wonderful served with sautéed spinach and a glass of crisp, dry white wine.

Serves 2

150 ml (¼ pint) milk
50 ml (2 fl oz) double cream
2 x 100 g (4 oz) haddock fillets,
    skinned and boned
2 tsp olive oil
1 small red onion, finely chopped
2 ripe firm tomatoes, seeded
    and diced
1 garlic clove, crushed
2 egg yolks
50 g (2 oz) freshly grated Parmesan
salt and freshly ground black pepper

Preheat the grill. Place the milk and cream in a wide pan and bring almost to the boil. Add the haddock fillets, reduce the heat and poach for 4–5 minutes until just tender.

Meanwhile, heat the oil in a frying pan and sauté the red onion for a few minutes until softened but not coloured. Add the tomatoes and garlic and continue to sauté for another 2 minutes. Season to taste and divide between warmed heatproof plates. Keep warm.

Remove the haddock from the poaching liquid and arrange on top of the tomato mixture. Keep warm.

Season the remaining poaching liquid and whisk in the egg yolks. Continue to cook for 1–2 minutes until thickened, stirring constantly. Stir in the Parmesan and ladle over the haddock to cover completely. Place the plates directly under the grill for 1–2 minutes until bubbling and lightly golden. Serve at once.

Monte Carlo or bust

Tony Tobin
GRIDDLED LIME AND CHILLI PRAWNS WITH MANGO SALSA

Tiger prawns are full of flavour, even if frozen. They cook in no time on a griddle pan and are perfect with a mango salsa, bursting with freshness.

Serves 2

10 large raw tiger prawns, peeled but
   tails intact, thawed if frozen
juice 1 lime
pinch dried crushed chillies
a little olive oil

FOR THE MANGO SALSA
3 small yellow peppers
1 small mango
4 spring onions, finely chopped
2 tbsp chopped mixed fresh herbs
   (such as flat-leaf parsley, mint
   and coriander)
finely grated rind and juice 1 lime
1 tbsp olive oil
Maldon sea salt and freshly ground
   black pepper

To make the salsa, scorch the skins of the peppers with a blowtorch and, when cool enough to handle, peel off the skins, cut the peppers in half, remove the seeds and dice the flesh. Place in a bowl. Peel the mango and dice the flesh, discarding the stone. Add to the peppers with the spring onions, herbs, lime rind and juice, olive oil and a pinch of salt. Stir to combine and set aside to allow the flavours to develop.

Heat a griddle pan until searing hot. Butterfly the prawns by splitting each one down the centre, keeping the tails intact. Place in a bowl and add the lime juice and dried chillies, tossing to coat. Drizzle a thin film of olive oil onto the griddle pan and add the prawns. Cook for 20–30 seconds on each side until lightly charred but still tender.

Arrange on plates with the mango salsa alongside to serve.

Nick Nairn
SMOKED SALMON WITH BAKED EGGS

A simple but effective meeting of three ingredients. It's more of a brunch or late supper dish than a main course. Serve with buttered toast soldiers for a retro feel.

Serves 2

25 g (1 oz) butter
225 g (8 oz) smoked salmon slices
   (about 8 in total)
225 ml (8 fl oz) double cream
4 eggs
freshly ground black pepper
crusty bread, to serve

Preheat the oven to 220°C/425°F/Gas 7. Grease two small gratin dishes with the butter. Ruffle up the salmon slices and divide them between the dishes.

Drizzle the double cream on top of the salmon and then break two eggs into each dish. Add a good grinding of black pepper and bake for 6–8 minutes or until the whites of the eggs are just set but the yolks are still runny.

Transfer the gratin dishes directly onto plates and arrange some crusty bread alongside to serve.

Lesley Waters
SCENTED SEAFOOD CURRY

Use any selection of seafood or firm-fleshed fish for this deliciously fragrant curry.

Serves 2

1 cm (½ in) piece fresh root ginger, peeled and chopped

2 garlic cloves, chopped

1 mild red chilli, seeded and chopped

1 small bunch coriander, plus extra leaves to garnish

2 tsp sunflower oil

6 tbsp vegetable stock (from a cube is fine)

6 tbsp double cream

175 g (6 oz) squid, cleaned and sliced

175 g (6 oz) raw peeled tiger prawns

100 g (4 oz) small live clams, cleaned

275 g (10 oz) packet cooked Thai fragrant rice (or use leftover rice)

salt and freshly ground black pepper

Place the ginger, garlic, chilli and coriander in a mini food processor with a splash of water. Blend to form a smooth paste, adding another splash of water if necessary.

Heat the oil in a pan and tip in the ginger paste. Heat gently for a minute or two until fragrant, then pour in the vegetable stock and allow to bubble down by half. Stir in the cream and bring to a gentle simmer. Cook for 1–2 minutes until slightly reduced and thickened.

Fold the squid, prawns and clams into the scented cream mixture and season to taste. Cover with a lid and heat gently until the seafood is cooked through and the clams have opened; discard any that do not open.

Meanwhile, heat the rice according to packet instructions and divide between warmed plates. Ladle on the scented seafood curry and garnish with coriander leaves to serve.

Lesley Waters
COD WRAPPED IN BACON WITH TARRAGON

The combination of bacon and fish works really well with the creamy tarragon sauce. As an alternative to the streaky bacon, try pancetta or wafer-thin slices of Parma ham.

Serves 2

4 rindless streaky bacon rashers

1 lemon, halved, pips removed

2 x 150 g (5 oz) cod fillets, any bones removed

2 tbsp chopped fresh tarragon

2 tbsp olive oil

85 ml (3 fl oz) white wine

120 ml (4 fl oz) double cream

salt and freshly ground black pepper

Preheat the oven to 220°C/425°F/Gas 7. Heat an ovenproof frying pan. Using the back of a knife, stretch the bacon to double its original length. Squeeze a little lemon juice over the cod, sprinkle over a little tarragon, season generously and then wrap with the bacon to enclose completely.

Add the oil to the heated frying pan and add the wrapped cod fillets, presentation-side down. Cook for 1–2 minutes until the bacon is lightly golden, then transfer to the oven and bake for another 5–6 minutes or until the fish is cooked through and the bacon is golden brown.

Meanwhile, place the wine in a small pan and simmer for a few minutes until reduced by half. Add the remaining lemon juice and the double cream and allow to reduce down a little. Season to taste and stir in the rest of the tarragon. Divide the tarragon sauce between warmed plates and place the cod wrapped in bacon on top. Serve at once.

seafood

103

Ross Burden
PAN-FRIED SEA BASS WITH ASPARAGUS AND BABY PLUM TOMATOES

Sweet, oval-shaped baby plum tomatoes are even tinier than cherry tomatoes. They are perfect for eating as they are or for barely heating through, as suggested there.

Serves 2

100 g (4 oz) fine asparagus tips, trimmed
3 tbsp olive oil
2 x 175 g (6 oz) sea bass fillets, scaled and any bones removed
75 g (3 oz) baby plum tomatoes
1 tsp chopped fresh tarragon
½ lemon, pips removed
salt and freshly ground black pepper

Heat a heavy-based frying pan. Blanch the asparagus tips in a pan of boiling salted water for 1–2 minutes until just tender but still crisp. Drain and quickly refresh under cold running water to prevent further cooking. Set aside until needed.

Add a tablespoon of the olive oil to the heated frying pan. Quickly slash the skin of the sea bass fillets, season with salt and add to the pan, skin-side down. Cook for 2–3 minutes until the skin is crisp and lightly golden. Turn the fillets over and cook for another minute. Transfer to a warm plate. The flesh at this stage will be slightly underdone, but will continue to cook after you remove it from the heat. Keep warm.

Add the remaining oil to the frying pan and toss in the asparagus and baby plum tomatoes. Season to taste and cook for 2–3 minutes until heated through, tossing constantly. Sprinkle over the tarragon and add a squeeze of lemon juice.

Spoon the asparagus and cherry tomato mixture onto warmed plates and arrange the fish neatly on top, skin-side up. Serve at once.

Paul Rankin
LINGUINE WITH CLAMS AND WHITE WINE

There is a wide array of clams now available from good fishmongers. Look out for amandes de mer, palourdes and tellines, or experiment with a mixture.

Serves 2

175 g (6 oz) linguine pasta
1 tbsp olive oil
1 small red onion, finely chopped
2 garlic cloves, finely chopped
85 ml (3 fl oz) dry white wine
1 ripe tomato, diced
good pinch dried crushed chillies
225 g (8 oz) live clams, well cleaned
1–2 tbsp extra-virgin olive oil
1 tbsp chopped fresh flat-leaf parsley
salt and freshly ground black pepper

Plunge the linguine into a pan of boiling salted water and cook for about 8 minutes until al dente, or according to the packet instructions.

Meanwhile, heat the oil in a large pan. Add the red onion and garlic and sauté for 2–3 minutes until softened but not coloured.

Pour the wine into the pan and allow to reduce right down, then tip in the tomato and add the crushed chillies. Bring to a simmer and boil fast for 1–2 minutes until slightly reduced. Season to taste.

Tip the clams into the pan, then cover with a tight-fitting lid and steam for 2–3 minutes, shaking the pan occasionally until all the clams have opened. Discard any that do not.

Meanwhile, drain the linguine. When the clams are cooked, add the linguine to the pan with a good glug of extra-virgin olive oil and toss until well combined. Divide between warmed wide-rimmed bowls, scatter over the parsley and serve.

'Clam rock'

Gino D'Acampo
CRISP FRIED LEMON SOLE WITH HERB VINAIGRETTE

I'd serve this with a fresh green salad and a glass of chilled white wine – perfect for a summer's evening. If you fancy a change from lemon sole, use any flat fish, such as plaice or turbot.

Serves 2

2 eggs
2 tbsp milk
25 g (1 oz) freshly grated Parmesan
2 tbsp mixed fresh chopped herbs (such as flat-leaf parsley, chives and basil)
pinch paprika
1 tbsp olive oil
knob butter
2 large lemon sole fillets

FOR THE HERB VINAIGRETTE
1 tsp white wine vinegar
squeeze lemon juice
2 tbsp extra-virgin olive oil
2 tbsp chopped mixed fresh herbs
salt and freshly ground black pepper

Heat a large frying pan. Break the eggs into a shallow dish and add the milk, Parmesan, herbs and paprika. Season to taste and whisk lightly to combine.

Add the olive oil and butter to the heated frying pan. Dip the lemon sole fillets into the egg mixture until well coated, gently shaking off any excess. Cook for 2–3 minutes on each side until the fish is cooked through and golden brown.

Meanwhile, make the herb vinaigrette. Place the vinegar and lemon juice in a bowl and whisk in a pinch of salt until dissolved. Gradually whisk in the olive oil until emulsified. Season with pepper and stir in the herbs.

Arrange the crisp fried lemon sole on warmed plates and drizzle the herb vinaigrette on top to serve.

Phil Vickery
PESTO SPAGHETTI WITH ANCHOVIES AND SUN-DRIED TOMATOES

This quick and delicious pasta dish is a great store-cupboard standby in our house. We normally have a basil plant on the kitchen windowsill, the only fresh ingredient you need for this.

Serves 2

225 g (8 oz) spaghetti
50 g (2 oz) can anchovies in olive oil, drained
2 garlic cloves
good handful fresh basil leaves
2 tsp sesame oil
4 tbsp olive oil
100 g (4 oz) sun-dried tomatoes preserved in oil, drained
100 g (4 oz) black olives
salt and freshly ground black pepper
freshly grated Parmesan, to serve

Plunge the spaghetti into a large pan of boiling salted water and cook for 8 minutes or according to packet instructions.

Meanwhile, make the pesto. Place two anchovies in a mini food processor with the garlic, basil and sesame and olive oils. Blend until smooth and season with black pepper. Finely chop the remaining anchovies and place in a large bowl. Cut the sun-dried tomatoes into thin strips and add to the bowl, along with the olives. Stir in the pesto.

Drain the spaghetti and then add to the bowl with the anchovy mixture, stirring to combine. Divide between warmed bowls and sprinkle Parmesan on top to serve.

poultry

Brian Turner
TANDOORI-STYLE CHICKEN WITH BUTTERED RICE

This may not be an authentic Indian-style tandoori, which takes days to make, but the results are incredibly good, particularly served with the buttery rice.

Serves 2

4 tbsp Greek yoghurt
1 tsp tomato purée
2 garlic cloves, crushed
3 cardamom pods, lightly crushed
1 tsp ground ginger
2 tsp medium curry powder
2 x 150 g (5 oz) skinless chicken
   fillets, cut into large cubes
2 tsp sunflower oil

FOR THE BUTTERED RICE
25 g (1 oz) butter
1 small onion, finely chopped
250 g (9 oz) packet cooked basmati
   rice (or use leftover rice)
4 tbsp hot chicken stock (from a
   cube is fine)
salt and freshly ground black pepper
chopped fresh coriander, to garnish

Preheat the oven to 200°C/400°F/Gas 6 and heat an ovenproof frying pan. Mix the yoghurt, tomato purée, garlic, cardamom, ginger and curry powder in a bowl. Add the chicken and stir until well coated.

Add the oil to the heated frying pan and then tip in the chicken. Quickly sauté for 1 minute to seal, then transfer to the oven and cook on the top shelf for 6–8 minutes until completely tender and lightly charred.

Meanwhile, make the buttered rice. Melt half the butter in a pan and sauté the onion over high heat for 1–2 minutes until softened. Add the rice and allow to just warm through, then sprinkle over the stock, tossing the pan constantly. Season to taste.

Generously grease six 150 ml (¼ pint) metal dariole moulds with the rest of the butter. Divide the rice among them and arrange on a baking sheet, then cover each one tightly with foil. Place on the second shelf in the oven and cook for another 2–3 minutes until all the stock has been absorbed.

To serve, pile the tandoori-style chicken in the middle of warmed plates and turn out three of the dariole moulds onto each plate. Garnish with the coriander.

' It takes two to tandoori '

James Martin

CREAMY CARDAMOM CHICKEN WITH CHILLI FLATBREADS

This mildly spiced curry is delicious served with the chilli flatbreads, which should be torn and dipped in to mop up every last bit. Skinless, boneless chicken thighs or turkey breast steaks would also work well.

Serves 2

2 tbsp sunflower oil

225 g (8 oz) skinless chicken breast
    fillets, chopped

1 red onion, thinly sliced

2 garlic cloves, finely chopped

1 tsp cardamom pods

1 tsp ground turmeric

1 tsp ground coriander

½ tsp ground ginger

100 ml (3½ fl oz) hot chicken stock

200 ml (7 fl oz) double cream

juice 1 lemon

FOR THE CHILLI FLATBREADS

150 g (5 oz) plain flour, plus extra
    for dusting

1 tbsp olive oil

finely grated rind of 1 lemon

2 tsp dried crushed chillies

salt and freshly ground black pepper

fresh coriander sprigs, to garnish
    (optional)

Heat a large flat griddle or cast-iron frying pan. Heat the sunflower oil in a sauté pan, add the chicken and sauté for 1–2 minutes until sealed. Tip in the onion and garlic and continue to cook for 1–2 minutes until golden.

Meanwhile, lightly crush the cardamom pods so that the green husks split open, then remove the little black seeds from inside. Grind these to a fine powder and sprinkle over the chicken and onion mixture along with the turmeric, coriander and ginger, and cook for 1–2 minutes, stirring.

Pour the stock into the pan with the cream and lemon juice. Season to taste and cook for another 3 minutes until the chicken is cooked through and the sauce has slightly reduced and thickened.

Meanwhile, make the chilli flatbreads. Place the flour in a large bowl with the oil, lemon rind and chilli, and pour in enough water to bind – you'll need about 4 tablespoons in total. Shape into a ball, then cut in two and roll each piece into a 10 cm (4 in) circle on a lightly floured surface.

Place both flatbreads on the heated flat griddle and cook for 1 minute on each side – you can speed up the cooking process by cooking the top with a blowtorch.

Spoon the creamy cardamom chicken into bowls set on plates and tuck the chilli flatbreads alongside. Garnish with coriander sprigs if liked, and serve at once.

Brian Turner
CHICKEN ESCALOPES WITH LEMON PARSLEY BUTTER

Simple, but very stylish, this dish would be excellent as a main course for a special supper. If time allows, the escalopes can be prepared in advance, ready to be cooked at the last minute.

Serves 2

50 g (2 oz) freshly grated Parmesan
50 g (2 oz) fresh white breadcrumbs
25 g (1 oz) seasoned flour
2 eggs
2 large skinless boneless chicken
   thighs, well trimmed
4 tbsp olive oil

FOR THE LEMON PARSLEY BUTTER

50 g (2 oz) unsalted butter
juice ½ lemon
1 tbsp chopped fresh flat-leaf parsley
salt and freshly ground black pepper
Crushed New Potatoes with Spring
   Onions, to serve (optional –
   see page 72)

Preheat the oven to 200°C/400°F/Gas 6 and heat a large ovenproof frying pan. Mix together the Parmesan and breadcrumbs in a shallow dish and season to taste. Place the seasoned flour on a flat plate. Beat the eggs and some seasoning in a shallow bowl.

Place the chicken thighs between two pieces of cling film and, using a rolling pin, flatten out to a 0.5 cm (¼ in) thickness. Toss in the seasoned flour, shaking off any excess, then dip in the beaten egg. Coat in the breadcrumbs, and then repeat with the egg and breadcrumbs.

Add the oil to the heated frying pan and fry the escalopes for 2 minutes on each side until lightly golden. Transfer the frying pan to the oven and continue to cook for another 4 minutes until completely tender and cooked through.

Meanwhile, make the lemon parsley butter. Melt the butter in a small frying pan. Before it begins to brown add the lemon juice and parsley, stirring to combine.

Arrange the escalopes on warmed plates and drizzle the lemon parsley butter on top. Serve at once with the Crushed New Potatoes, if liked.

James Martin
CHICKEN CHIMICHANGAS

These delicious chimichangas are simply deep-fried Mexican tortillas. I normally have a packet of large tortillas in the cupboard – they often come in handy. An avocado and tomato salsa wouldn't go amiss either.

Serves 2

sunflower oil, for deep-frying
2 tbsp olive oil
100 g (4 oz) skinless chicken breast
    fillets, thinly sliced
2 garlic cloves, finely chopped
½ tsp dried crushed chillies
6 pepperdew peppers, drained and
    sliced (from a jar)
4 baby courgettes, thinly sliced
    on the diagonal
2 tbsp roughly chopped
    fresh coriander
juice 1 lime
2 large soft flour tortillas
1 Little Gem lettuce, shredded
4 tbsp soured cream
paprika, for dusting
salt and freshly ground black pepper
lime wedges, to serve

Preheat a deep-fat fryer or fill a deep-sided pan one-third full with oil and heat to 190°F/375°F. If you don't have a thermometer, the oil should be hot enough so that when a bread cube is added, it browns in 40 seconds.

Heat the olive oil in a frying pan and sauté the chicken, garlic and chillies for a few minutes over a high heat until lightly golden. Season to taste. Add the peppers and courgettes and continue to sauté for 2–3 minutes until tender. Fold in the coriander and lime juice, then remove from the heat.

Meanwhile, warm the tortillas in a hot, dry frying pan until soft and flexible. Spoon half of the chicken mixture into the centre of each tortilla and fold over the edges to form a neat parcel, then fix in place with wooden cocktail sticks.

Deep-fry the chimichangas for 2 minutes until golden brown, then drain well on kitchen paper and slice on the diagonal. Pile the shredded lettuce onto plates and arrange the chimichangas on top. Add a good dollop of soured cream to the side and dust with paprika. Garnish with lime wedges to serve.

poultry

113

Paul Rankin
CHICKEN SATAY WITH DIPPING SAUCE AND CUCUMBER SALAD

It's always good to be able to do a quick and simple version of a classic dish. You could marinate the chicken for up to 24 hours, if time allows.

Serves 2

2 tbsp dark soy sauce
1 tsp clear honey
1 tsp medium curry powder
225 g (8 oz) skinless chicken fillets,
    cut into long strips
4 tbsp rice wine vinegar
2 tbsp caster sugar
½ small cucumber, peeled, halved,
    seeded and thinly sliced

FOR THE DIPPING SAUCE
2 tbsp crunchy peanut butter
2 tsp dark soy sauce
1 tsp light muscovado sugar
juice ½ lime
120 ml/4 fl oz coconut milk
½ mild red chilli, seeded and
    finely diced
2 tbsp chopped fresh coriander
salt and freshly ground black pepper

Heat a griddle pan until very hot. Whisk together the soy sauce, honey and curry powder. Season with pepper and add the chicken pieces. Leave to marinate for 2 minutes.

Thread the chicken pieces onto six 15 cm (6 in) bamboo skewers and arrange on the griddle pan. Cook for 4–6 minutes until completely tender and cooked through, turning once or twice.

Meanwhile, prepare the cucumber salad. Place the vinegar in a bowl and stir in the sugar and a good pinch of salt until dissolved. Tip in the cucumber, stirring to combine, and set aside to allow the flavours to develop.

To make the dipping sauce, put the peanut butter in a bowl and stir in the soy sauce, light muscovado sugar and lime juice. Gradually whisk in the coconut milk until you have achieved a smooth sauce. Stir in the chilli and coriander, then divide between individual dipping bowls.

Divide the cucumber salad between individual serving bowls, leaving behind any excess liquid. Arrange the chicken satay skewers on plates with both bowls to the side and serve at once.

Ross Burden
CHICKEN AND NOODLE GORENG

This is a version of Indonesian stir-fried noodles that I often find myself cooking at home using up whatever is left over in the fridge. For authenticity use sambal oelek (Indonesian red chilli paste) and ketjap manis (Indonesian sweet soy sauce), but this recipe works extremely well with more accessible store-cupboard ingredients.

Serves 2

2 tbsp sunflower oil
2 spring onions, finely chopped
2 tsp freshly grated root ginger
2 garlic cloves, finely chopped
225 g (8 oz) skinless boneless chicken thighs, well trimmed and cut into small, thin strips
1 onion, thinly sliced
50 g (2 oz) baby carrots, thinly sliced on the diagonal
100 g (4 oz) baby courgettes, trimmed and sliced on the diagonal
100 g (4 oz) medium egg noodles
1 tbsp dark soy sauce
1 tsp clear honey
¼ tsp chilli powder
½ tsp ground turmeric
2 tsp chopped fresh coriander

Heat a wok until very hot, then swirl in the oil. Add the spring onions, ginger and garlic to the wok and stir-fry for 20 seconds. Tip in the chicken and continue to stir-fry for a minute or two until it is sealed and lightly golden.

Add the onion, baby carrots and courgettes to the wok and continue to stir-fry for another 3–4 minutes until all the vegetables are just tender, sprinkling over a tablespoon of water if the mixture is getting too dry.

Meanwhile, place the noodles in a pan of boiling water and simmer for 3 minutes or according to packet instructions. Place the soy sauce, honey, chilli powder, turmeric and coriander in a large bowl and mix well until smooth. Drain the noodles and tip them straight into the soy mixture, tossing quickly until evenly coated.

Add the stir-fried chicken and vegetables to the flavoured noodles and mix again until evenly combined. Divide between warmed plates and serve at once.

James Tanner
SESAME, SOY AND LIME CHICKEN SKEWERS

These skewers are full of fresh, clean flavours; the sauce is similar to teriyaki but not quite as sweet.

Serves 2

225 g (8 oz) skinless chicken fillet, cut into 2 cm (¾ in) cubes

1 red romero pepper, halved, seeded and cut into 2 cm (¾ in) cubes

1 small courgette, sliced on the diagonal

1 small red onion, cut into 2 cm (¾ in) pieces

juice 1 lime

2 tbsp dark soy sauce

juice ½ orange

1 tbsp sesame oil

pinch caster sugar

250 g (9 oz) packet cooked basmati rice

Heat a flat griddle pan until very hot. Meanwhile, place the chicken in a large bowl with the red pepper, courgette and onion pieces. Add the lime juice, soy sauce, orange juice, sesame oil and sugar. Toss until well combined and then thread onto six 15 cm (6 in) bamboo skewers.

Add the chicken skewers to the heated griddle pan and sear on all sides for about 1 minute, then reduce the heat and cook for another minute or so on each side until the chicken and vegetables are cooked through and tender.

Meanwhile, place the remaining marinade in a small pan and cook for about 5 minutes until well reduced and sticky.

Heat the rice according to packet instructions. Divide between warmed plates and arrange the chicken skewers to the side. Drizzle over the reduced marinade and serve at once.

Antony Worrall Thompson
TURKEY STROGANOFF WITH HERB RICE

For evenings when you want instant comfort food, you can't go far wrong with this variation on an old favourite.

Serves 2

100 g (4 oz) quick-cook long-grain rice

2 tbsp olive oil

1 small red onion, thinly sliced

2 x 75 g (3 oz) turkey breast steaks, cut into strips

1 tsp hot paprika, plus extra for dusting

50 g (2 oz) button chestnut mushrooms, thinly sliced

good glug dry white wine

50 ml (2 fl oz) double cream

2 tbsp chopped mixed fresh herbs (such as chives, basil and flat-leaf parsley)

knob butter

2 tbsp Greek yoghurt

salt and freshly ground black pepper

Cook the rice in a pan of boiling salted water for 8–10 minutes until tender.

Meanwhile, heat the oil in a frying pan and cook the onion for 1–2 minutes until softened, stirring constantly. Toss the turkey in the paprika and then add to the pan. Cook for another few minutes until sealed and lightly golden.

Tip the mushrooms into the pan and continue to cook for 1 minute, tossing until well combined. Pour in the wine and allow it to bubble down, then add the cream, stirring to combine. Season to taste and allow to simmer for another minute or two until slightly thickened and reduced.

Drain the rice and return to the pan, then stir in the herbs and butter. Divide between warmed plates and spoon the turkey stroganoff alongside. Add a dollop of yoghurt to each and finish with a dusting of paprika to serve.

poultry

117

Nick Nairn
CHAR-GRILLED CHICKEN WITH COUSCOUS AND HERB SALAD

I use an American gadget called a microplane grater to pare the rind effortlessly from the lemon, leaving behind the bitter pith – it has become my favourite kitchen gadget.

Serves 2

2 skinless chicken breast fillets,
 thinly sliced
1 garlic clove, crushed
1 small hot red chilli, seeded and
 finely chopped
5 tbsp olive oil
1 lemon
175 ml (6 fl oz) hot chicken stock
 (from a cube is fine)
150 g (5 oz) couscous
1 small red onion, finely diced
1 small red pepper, halved, seeded
 and very finely diced
good handful mixed fresh herbs,
 such as chives, flat-leaf parsley
 and basil leaves
a little balsamic vinegar
1 tbsp extra-virgin olive oil
salt and freshly ground black pepper

Place the chicken in a bowl with the garlic, chilli, two tablespoons of the olive oil and seasoning. Pare in the lemon rind and mix well to combine, then set aside to marinate.

Meanwhile, bring the stock to the boil in a small pan and then pour in the couscous in a thin, steady stream, mixing well until all the stock is absorbed. Season to taste and fold in the red onion and pepper. Cover, remove from the heat and leave for 3 minutes.

Heat a heavy-based frying pan until searing hot. Flash fry the marinated chicken pieces for a few minutes until cooked through and lightly browned. Squeeze over the juice from half of the lemon. Tip out onto kitchen paper to drain.

Remove the lid from the couscous and stir in the remaining olive oil and squeeze over the juice from the rest of the lemon.

Spoon the couscous into the centre of warmed plates and scatter the chicken over. Place all the herbs in a bowl and dress with a little balsamic vinegar and a dash of the extra-virgin olive oil. Finish with a pile of the herb salad on top, and drizzle the rest of the extra-virgin olive oil around the plates to serve.

Nick Nairn
CHICKEN AND NOODLE STIR-FRY

This stir-fry is fresh-tasting and full of zingy and spicy flavours. Egg noodles are one of the great store-cupboard standbys and need only four minutes' soaking in boiling water.

Serves 2

100 g (4 oz) medium egg noodles
1 tsp sesame seeds
2 tbsp sunflower oil
1 shallot, thinly sliced
1 small red pepper, halved, seeded and thinly sliced
1 skinless chicken breast fillet, thinly sliced on the diagonal
juice 1 lime
1 tbsp clear honey
1 tbsp dark soy sauce
1 tbsp sesame oil
good pinch dried crushed chillies
1 pak choi, thinly sliced on the diagonal
1 tbsp cornflour, mixed with a little water

Drop the noodles into a pan of boiling water and remove from the heat. Stir with a fork and then leave to stand for 4 minutes or according to packet instructions until tender. Stir again and drain well. Toast the sesame seeds in a small dry frying pan, tossing occasionally to ensure they colour evenly.

Meanwhile, heat a wok until very hot. Add the sunflower oil, swirling it up the sides of the wok, then tip in the shallot, pepper and chicken and stir-fry for a few minutes until the chicken is lightly browned.

Stir the lime juice into the chicken mixture with the honey, soy sauce, sesame oil and crushed chillies and continue to stir-fry for another few minutes until nicely glazed.

Add the pak choi to the wok with the cornflour mixture and heat gently for 2–3 minutes, stirring occasionally until the chicken has cooked through and a nice sauce has formed. Fold in the noodles and allow to completely warm through, then divide between serving bowls and sprinkle over the toasted sesame seeds to serve.

Gino D'Acampo
PARMA-WRAPPED CHICKEN
WITH CAMBOZOLA

This would also be delicious served on a bed of Creamed Sweet Potatoes
(see page 73) instead of the tomato salad.

Serves 2

2 skinless boneless chicken thighs,
 well trimmed
100 g (4 oz) cambozola cheese,
 rind removed and cut into two
 even-sized pieces
4 thin slices Parma ham
2 tbsp olive oil
25 g (1 oz) unsalted butter
100 ml (4 fl oz) double cream
50 g (2 oz) freshly grated Parmesan
2 plum tomatoes, sliced
1 tsp snipped fresh chives
few drops balsamic vinegar
dash extra-virgin olive oil
salt and freshly ground black pepper

Preheat the oven to 220°C/425°F/Gas 7 and heat an ovenproof frying pan.
Open out each chicken thigh and place between two pieces of cling film,
then flatten out with a rolling pin. Add a grinding of black pepper to each
one and place a piece of the cambozola in the middle. Fold over to
enclose the filling completely, then wrap each one with two slices of the
Parma ham.

Add the oil to the heated frying pan and then add the chicken parcels.
Cook over a high heat for 30 seconds or so on each side to seal
completely, then transfer to the oven and cook for another 6–8 minutes or
until the chicken is cooked through and tender.

Meanwhile, make the Parmesan cream. Melt the butter in a small pan.
Add the cream and Parmesan and season with pepper. Simmer gently for
3–4 minutes until the Parmesan has melted, stirring occasionally. Keep
warm over a low heat.

Arrange the tomatoes in an overlapping layer round the edge of each
serving plate. Scatter over the chives and season generously, then drizzle
over a little balsamic vinegar and extra-virgin olive oil. Drizzle the
Parmesan cream in the middle of each plate and top with the chicken
parcels to serve.

poultry

121

meat

Nick Nairn
SIZZLING SPAGHETTI CARBONARA

This isn't the easiest recipe in the world to get done in ten minutes, but it is achievable. The secret lies in getting the pasta dough just right – too much flour and it will be dry and crack when you roll it out; too little and the dough will be soft and stick to itself.

Serves 2

1 tbsp olive oil
6 thin slices pancetta (Italian streaky bacon)
4 tbsp double cream
4 tbsp freshly grated Parmesan, plus extra to garnish
2 egg yolks
handful fresh basil leaves, roughly torn

FOR THE PASTA DOUGH
200 g (7 oz) Italian '00' flour
2 eggs
salt and freshly ground black pepper

Bring a large pan of salted water to a rolling boil. To make the pasta dough, place the flour in a food processor and start it whizzing round. Add the eggs and keep whizzing until the mixture resembles fine breadcrumbs (it shouldn't be dusty, nor should it be a big gooey ball). Knead briskly into a ball shape and cut into two pieces.

Pass one piece of the pasta dough through a pasta machine set at its widest setting. Repeat this process, decreasing the roller setting grade by grade with each pass, taking it down to the second-lowest setting. Finally, pass through the cutting rollers to make spaghetti. Repeat with the remaining piece of dough.

Meanwhile, heat the olive oil in a frying pan. Add the pancetta and cook for about 2 minutes on each side until crisp and golden brown. Drain well on kitchen paper.

Plunge the pasta into the pan of boiling salted water and cook for 2–3 minutes until al dente. Place the cream in a bowl with the Parmesan and egg yolks and stir well to combine. Season to taste.

When the spaghetti is cooked, quickly drain in a colander and then return to the pan off the heat. Add the cream mixture and stir until heated through and thickened.

Divide between warmed wide-rimmed bowls and arrange crispy pancetta slices on top. Scatter over the basil and garnish with Parmesan to serve.

meat

123

‘ Fasta with the pasta ’

Ross Burden
CRISPY PORK LETTUCE ROLLS

This delicious Asian-inspired crispy pork rolled up in crisp lettuce leaves with a
scattering of fresh aromatic herbs is a very healthy option. ▶

Serves 2

2 garlic cloves, finely chopped
good pinch dried crushed chillies
juice 1 lime
2 tbsp chopped fresh coriander
1 tbsp sunflower oil
225 g (8 oz) lean minced pork
1 small iceberg lettuce
1 carrot
2 tbsp light soy sauce
1 tbsp clear honey
good handful mixed fresh herb leaves
    (such as coriander, basil and mint)
salt and freshly ground black pepper

Heat a large frying pan or wok. Mix the garlic, chillies, half a teaspoon
each of salt and pepper, the lime juice and coriander in a small bowl.

Add the oil to the wok, then tip in the garlic mixture and stir-fry for 20
seconds. Add the pork and stir-fry for 6–8 minutes until well browned and
crispy, breaking up the mince as it cooks with a wooden spoon.

Meanwhile, separate the iceberg lettuce into leaves, discarding any outer
damaged ones. Trim down to an even size with scissors – you'll need about
eight in total – and set aside until needed. Shred the carrot on a mandolin.

Add the soy sauce to the wok with the honey and cook for another minute
until the liquid has almost completely evaporated, stirring occasionally.
Serve in individual dishes so that you and your guest can spoon the pork
mixture into the lettuce leaves and scatter the carrot and fresh herb
leaves on top before rolling up to eat.

Ross Burden
PORK PATTIES WITH SPICED COCONUT CREAM

These would be fantastic on the barbecue. You could also make them with minced lamb or beef.

Serves 2

2 tbsp sunflower oil
1 small red onion, finely chopped
1 garlic clove, crushed
1 small bunch fresh coriander
    (roots intact)
¼ tsp ground coriander
¼ tsp ground cumin
1 tsp tomato purée
½ tsp medium curry powder
250 ml (8½ fl oz) packet
    coconut cream
175 g (6 oz) lean minced pork
275 g (10 oz) packet cooked basmati rice
salt and freshly ground black pepper

Heat a heavy-based frying pan. Put half the oil in a separate pan, add the
onion and garlic and sauté for 2–3 minutes until softened but not coloured.

Meanwhile, place the fresh coriander, ground coriander, cumin, tomato
purée and curry powder in a mini blender and blitz to a fine paste.

Add the paste to the sautéed onion mixture, stirring to combine, then
gradually add the coconut cream. Simmer for another 4–5 minutes until
slightly reduced and thickened.

Meanwhile, prepare the pork and the rice. Season the pork and shape into
10 even-sized patties. Add the remaining oil to the heated heavy-based
frying pan and cook for 6–8 minutes until cooked through and golden
brown. Heat the rice in the microwave according to packet instructions.

Divide the rice between warmed plates. Arrange the pork patties alongside
and pour over the spiced coconut cream to cover completely. Serve at once.

Brian Turner
SHEPHERD'S PIE

For a rich, tasty, succulent winter warmer, look no further. Cooking this in ten minutes was really pushing it – had I had an extra couple of minutes, I would have flashed the potato topping under the grill for a golden finish.

Serves 2

300 g (10 oz) potatoes, chopped into
    small pieces
1 tbsp olive oil
225 g (8 oz) lamb steak, trimmed
    and diced
2 tbsp finely chopped onion
1 large carrot, finely diced
175 g (6 oz) frozen peas
1 tbsp tomato ketchup
1 tsp Dijon mustard
dash Worcestershire sauce
50 ml (2 fl oz) hot lamb stock
    (from a cube is fine)
40 g (1½ oz) butter
1 tbsp double cream
salt and freshly ground black pepper

Place the potatoes in a pan of boiling salted water and bring to the boil, then reduce the heat and simmer for 8 minutes until completely tender.

Meanwhile, heat the oil in a frying pan. Add the lamb, onion and carrot and sauté for 2–3 minutes until the lamb is browned and the onion has softened.

Place the peas in a pan of boiling salted water and simmer for 4–5 minutes until tender.

Stir the tomato ketchup into the lamb mixture with the mustard and Worcestershire sauce and then pour in the stock. Season to taste. Continue to cook for another couple of minutes until the mixture is quite thick and dry and the carrots are tender.

Place a 10 cm (4 in) metal cooking ring on each warmed plate and divide the lamb mixture between them. Drain the peas and toss in a small knob of the butter. Quickly drain the potatoes and mash with the rest of the butter and the cream. Spoon the mash over the lamb mixture to cover completely and then smooth the top with a palette knife. Carefully remove the metal rings and serve at once with buttered peas.

Lesley Waters
CHIPOLATAS WITH SKILLET SCONES AND ROASTED TOMATOES

My kids go crazy for this dish. The skillet scones are best eaten as soon as they come off the pan. If you want to keep them for any longer, sprinkle over a little water and wrap in a clean tea towel to prevent the crusts becoming hard.

Serves 2

5 small vine-ripened tomatoes, halved
olive oil, for drizzling
10 chipolata sausages

FOR THE SKILLET SCONES
100 g (4 oz) self-raising flour, plus
   extra for dusting
2 tbsp finely chopped red onion
1 tbsp snipped fresh chives
1 tbsp olive oil, plus extra for cooking
100 ml (3½ fl oz) milk
salt and freshly ground black pepper
butter, to serve (optional)

Preheat the oven to 200°C/400°F/Gas 6. Place the tomatoes in a baking tin and drizzle over a little olive oil. Season generously and bake for 8–9 minutes until lightly charred and softened.

Heat a flat griddle or skillet pan until hot. Place the flour in a bowl with the red onion, chives and a pinch of salt. Make a well in the centre and pour in the olive oil and milk. Quickly bring the mixture together to a soft dough.

Turn the dough out onto a lightly floured board and knead lightly until smooth. Roll out to a 2 cm (¾ in) thickness and stamp out 5 cm (2 in) circles with a fluted pastry cutter. Add a thin film of oil to the flat griddle pan and cook the scones for 2–3 minutes on each side until slightly risen and golden brown.

Add the chipolata sausages to the griddle pan and cook for about 6 minutes until golden brown and cooked through, turning occasionally.

Split the scones and spread with butter, if liked, then arrange on warmed plates with the roasted tomatoes and chipolatas to serve.

' No scone unturned '

meat

127

Tony Tobin
SAUSAGES AND MASH WITH ONION GRAVY

This is comfort food at its best, satisfying and easy to prepare. The creamy, super-quick mash is made with butter beans. Serve with the best sausages you can find. ◄

Serves 2

sunflower oil for brushing
6 pork and leek sausages
25 g (1 oz) butter
1 red onion, thinly sliced
about 85 ml (3 fl oz) red wine

FOR THE MASH

25 g (1 oz) butter
1 small onion, finely chopped
400 g (14 oz) can butter beans, drained and rinsed
2 tbsp hot chicken stock (from a cube is fine)
splash double cream
salt and freshly ground black pepper

Heat a griddle pan until hot, brush with oil and add the sausages, then cook for 6–8 minutes until completely tender and nicely marked.

Meanwhile, make the onion gravy. Melt a knob of the butter in a pan and sauté the red onion for about 5 minutes until softened and just beginning to colour. Season to taste. To make the mash, heat the butter in a pan and gently fry the onion for 2–3 minutes until softened but not coloured. Stir in the butter beans and heat through. Stir in the stock and cream, warm through, then season to taste. Blitz with a hand blender to a thick, smooth purée, adding a little more cream if necessary.

To finish the gravy, pour the wine into the onion mixture and allow to cook down for a couple of minutes until reduced by half. Whisk the remaining butter into the gravy.

Arrange the sausages on warmed plates with the mash and spoon the gravy on top. Serve at once.

James Martin
PAN-FRIED PORK ESCALOPE WITH MUSTARD AND DILL

Good quality pork will have a degree of fat that helps soften the meat during cooking.

Serves 2

250 g (9 oz) baby new potatoes, halved
2 tbsp olive oil
2 pork escalopes
300 ml (½ pint) double cream
1 tsp wholegrain mustard
1 tbsp chopped fresh dill
50 g (2 oz) freshly grated Parmesan
salt and freshly ground black pepper

Cook the potatoes in a pan of boiling salted water for about 8 minutes until tender.

Meanwhile, heat the olive oil in a frying pan. Season the pork escalopes and then sauté for 4–5 minutes until tender, turning once. Remove from the heat and keep warm. Return the frying pan to the heat and deglaze with the cream and mustard. Reduce the heat and continue to cook for a few minutes until nicely reduced and thickened. Season to taste and stir in the dill.

Drain the cooked potatoes and return to the pan, then coarsely crush with a potato masher. Stir in the Parmesan and season with plenty of pepper. Spoon the crushed Parmesan potatoes onto warmed plates and add the pork escalopes. Spoon over the mustard and dill sauce to serve.

meat

Antony Worrall Thompson
LAMB KOFTAS

If you don't have a flat griddle pan, cook the koftas under the grill, but soak the bamboo skewers in water first to prevent them from catching alight.

Serves 2

225 g (8 oz) lean minced lamb
1 garlic clove, roughly chopped
1 tsp hot paprika
½ tsp chilli powder
¼ tsp ground cinnamon
½ tsp ground cumin
¼ tsp ground ginger
1 egg
1 tbsp olive oil
2 white pitta breads
6 tbsp Greek yoghurt
1 small ripe tomato, finely diced
5 cm (2 in) piece cucumber, halved,
    seeded and finely diced
1 tbsp chopped fresh flat-leaf parsley
salt and freshly ground black pepper
lemon wedges, to garnish

Heat a large flat griddle pan and preheat the grill. Place the lamb mince in a food processor with the garlic, paprika, chilli powder, cinnamon, cumin, ginger and egg. Pulse until well combined and then divide into six portions. Squeeze round 15 cm (6 in) bamboo skewers to form kofta shapes.

Add the oil to the griddle pan and cook the koftas for 6–8 minutes, turning every 2 minutes or so to ensure they cook and colour evenly. Meanwhile, grill the pitta breads for about 30 seconds on each side until puffed up and lightly golden, then cut in half on the diagonal.

To make the dressing, place the yoghurt in a bowl with the tomato, cucumber and parsley. Season to taste and mix well to combine.

Arrange the koftas on warmed plates and drizzle over the yoghurt dressing. Add the pitta halves and garnish with lemon wedges to serve.

Tony Tobin
HAM AND MUSHROOM PUFF PIE

This crafty pie uses ready-made puff pastry and cooks it separately from the filling.

Serves 2

100 g (4 oz) ready-made puff pastry,
    thawed if frozen
a little plain flour, for dusting
1 egg, beaten with a little water
knob butter
1 tbsp olive oil
2 shallots, chopped
150 g (5 oz) wild mushrooms, sliced
good pinch fresh soft thyme leaves
splash dry white wine
50 ml (2 fl oz) double cream
175 g (6 oz) piece cooked ham,
    cut into cubes
salt and freshly ground black pepper

Preheat the oven to 220°C/425°F/Gas 7. Heat two non-stick frying pans. Roll out the puff pastry on a lightly floured board, cut out two 10 cm (4 in) discs and add to the heated frying pans. Cook for a minute or so, then flip over and brush with the egg mixture while cooking for another minute. Transfer to a non-stick baking sheet and bake for 7–8 minutes or until well risen and golden brown.

Meanwhile, heat the butter and oil in a frying pan and sauté the shallots for 1–2 minutes until softened but not coloured. Add the mushrooms and thyme and cook for another 2–3 minutes until tender. Season to taste. Pour the wine into the pan and allow to bubble right down. Pour in the cream, add the ham, then reduce the heat and simmer for another couple of minutes until the cream has slightly reduced and the ham is heated through.

Spoon the ham and mushroom mixture onto plates, piling it high, and arrange a pastry disc on top to serve.

Gino D'Acampo
TOAD-IN-THE-HOLE WITH SPICED BAKED BEANS

The blini pans need to be very hot to enable the puddings to rise quickly.

Serves 2

2 tsp sunflower oil
4 tbsp self-raising flour
pinch baking powder
1 egg
100 ml (3½ fl oz) milk
100 g (4 oz) cooked cocktail sausages
½ tsp fresh soft thyme leaves
200 g (7 oz) can baked beans
knob butter
splash double cream
pinch medium curry powder
salt and freshly ground black pepper

Preheat the oven to 220°C/425°F/Gas 7. Add a teaspoon of oil to two blini pans and heat in the oven.

To make the Yorkshire pudding batter, place the flour and baking powder in a large bowl with a pinch of salt. Make a well in the centre, break in the egg and gradually draw in the flour. Quickly add the milk and whisk vigorously into a smooth batter – the consistency of single cream. Transfer to a jug. Remove the hot blini pans from the oven and pour in enough batter to come halfway up the sides. Scatter the cocktail sausages and thyme over both pans, then bake on the top shelf of the oven for 8 minutes or until well risen and golden brown.

Meanwhile, pour the baked beans into a small pan and add the butter, cream and curry powder. Heat gently for 2–3 minutes until warmed through. Season to taste. Tip the toad-in-the-holes onto warmed plates and spoon over the spiced baked beans to serve.

Paul Rankin
CHORIZO STEW WITH BLACK OLIVES

I've made many variations of this stew over the years on *Ready Steady Cook* because the flavours work so well. If time allows, try a buttered herby breadcrumb topping and flash under the grill.

Serves 2

1 tbsp olive oil, plus extra for drizzling
1 hot red chilli, seeded and finely chopped
1 red onion, finely chopped
2 garlic cloves, crushed, plus 1 garlic clove, halved
100 g (4 oz) uncooked chorizo, diced
2 large thick slices rustic bread, such as sourdough
200 g (7 oz) can chopped tomatoes
1–2 tbsp tomato ketchup
400 g (14 oz) can black-eye beans, drained and rinsed
50 g (2 oz) pitted black olives
salt and freshly ground black pepper
handful chopped fresh flat-leaf parsley, to serve

Heat a griddle pan until very hot. Heat the oil in a large pan and sauté the chilli, red onion and crushed garlic for a few minutes until softened but not coloured.

Add the chorizo to the pan and season to taste, then continue to cook for 4–5 minutes until it is sizzling and has released some of its oil.

Meanwhile, add the slices of bread to the heated griddle pan and cook for 1–2 minutes on each side until lightly charred. Drizzle over a little olive oil and rub with the halved garlic clove.

Pour the tomatoes into the chorizo pan along with tomato ketchup to taste and the black-eye beans and olives, stirring to combine. Cook for 1–2 minutes until heated through. Season to taste.

Divide the chorizo stew between warmed bowls set on serving plates and scatter with parsley. Place the bruschetta on the side and serve at once.

Phil Vickery
VENISON BURGER WITH PRUNE SALAD

Here is a simple but rather unusual way of serving venison sausages. Most supermarkets now stock them, but better still, seek out a local butcher who makes his own.

Serves 2

4 venison sausages
2 spring onions, finely chopped
1 tsp chopped fresh thyme
4 prunes, stoned and finely chopped
olive oil, for cooking
2 ciabatta rolls

FOR THE PRUNE SALAD
handful fresh flat-leaf parsley leaves
handful fresh coriander leaves
small bunch fresh chives, roughly
    sliced on the diagonal
2 spring onions, finely sliced
2 prunes, stoned and chopped
1 tsp toasted sesame seeds
½ tsp white wine vinegar
1 tbsp extra-virgin olive oil
salt and freshly ground black pepper

Preheat the oven to 200°C/400°F/Gas 6 and heat an ovenproof frying pan. Split the skin on each venison sausage and place the meat in a bowl. Add the spring onions, thyme, prunes and seasoning. Mix together using your hands and then shape into two even-sized patties.

Add a thin film of olive oil to the heated frying pan and then quickly sear the venison patties on both sides. Transfer to the oven and cook for another 5–6 minutes or until cooked through and tender.

Heat a griddle pan until hot. Split the ciabatta rolls, drizzle with a little olive oil and toast on the griddle pan.

To make the prune salad, place the parsley in a bowl with the coriander, chives, spring onions, prunes, sesame seeds, vinegar and olive oil. Mix well to combine.

Place the bottom halves of the ciabatta rolls on warmed plates and top each one with a venison patty. Pile the prune salad on top and place the tops to the side to serve.

hot desserts

Lesley Waters
APPLE STRUDEL ROLLS WITH CARDAMOM CUSTARD

I was lucky enough to have authentic Greek filo pastry for this recipe – it is the easiest to handle and gives the best result.

Serves 2

sunflower oil, for deep-frying
50 g (2 oz) butter
good pinch ground ginger
good pinch ground cinnamon
finely grated rind of 1 lemon
1 apple, peeled, cored and diced
25 g (1 oz) sultanas
150 g (5 oz) filo pastry, thawed if frozen
1 egg, beaten

FOR THE CARDAMOM CUSTARD

150 ml (¼ pint) milk
2 egg yolks
1 tbsp caster sugar
1 cardamom pod, split open and seeds
   ground to a powder

Preheat a deep-fat fryer or fill a deep-sided pan one-third full with oil and heat to 190°F/375°F. If you don't have a thermometer, the oil should be hot enough so that when a bread cube is added, it browns in 40 seconds.

Melt the butter in a pan and pour half into a small bowl to use for the filo. Stir the ginger into the remainder with the cinnamon, lemon rind, apple and sultanas. Cook gently for 2–3 minutes until the apples are beginning to soften, stirring occasionally.

Meanwhile, cut the filo into six 25 cm (10 in) squares. Layer up three squares, lightly brushing with melted butter between each one. Spoon half of the apple mixture about 7.5 cm (3 in) from one of the corners. Pull over the corner to enclose the filling completely, then fold in the two sides and roll up like a cigar, using a little of the beaten egg to seal the edges. Repeat with the remaining filo and filling.

Deep-fry the strudel rolls in the heated oil for 2–3 minutes until crisp and golden brown. Carefully remove with a slotted spoon and drain well on kitchen paper.

Meanwhile, quickly make the cardamom custard. Heat the milk in a small pan but do not allow to boil. Whisk the egg yolks, sugar and cardamom in a bowl until pale and fluffy. Slowly pour in the hot milk, whisking constantly. Return the mixture to a clean pan and whisk over a gentle heat until thickened.

Arrange the apple strudel rolls on warmed plates and spoon over the cardamom custard to serve.

'I think you need oodles of strudel to live apple-y everafter'

hot desserts

Nick Nairn
GINGER SPONGE PUDDING WITH CUSTARD AND NUT BRITTLE

You need a larger pudding basin than you might think because the sponge needs room to expand during cooking.

Serves 2

100 g (4 oz) unsalted butter, plus
    extra for greasing
100 g (4 oz) self-raising flour
100 g (4 oz) caster sugar, plus a
    little extra
50 g (2 oz) crystallized ginger, finely
    chopped (from a jar)
1 tsp baking powder
2 eggs

FOR THE CUSTARD
150 ml (5 fl oz) milk
100 ml (3½ fl oz) double cream
1 vanilla pod, split in half and seeds
    scraped out
2 egg yolks
25 g (1 oz) caster sugar

FOR NUT BRITTLE
100 g (4 oz) caster sugar
25 g (1 oz) Brazil nuts

To make the sponge pudding, grease a 1.2 litre (2 pint) microwavable pudding basin with butter and sprinkle lightly with caster sugar, gently knocking out any excess. Place the butter, flour, sugar, crystallized ginger and baking powder in a food processor. Add the eggs and blend until smooth.

Transfer the sponge mixture to the prepared pudding basin – it should be no more than two-thirds full to allow the pudding to rise. Cover tightly with cling film. Pierce a couple of times with a sharp knife then cook on full power for 5 minutes until well risen and cooked through.

Meanwhile, make the custard. Place the milk, cream, scraped-out vanilla pod and seeds in a small pan and bring to a simmer. Remove from the heat and set aside to allow the flavours to infuse while you beat the egg yolks and sugar in a large bowl. Remove the vanilla pod from the milk mixture and gradually whisk into the egg mixture until well combined. Pour back into a clean pan and stir over a gentle heat for a couple of minutes until the custard has thickened and coats the back of a wooden spoon.

To make the nut brittle, place a small frying pan over a high heat. Add the caster sugar and Brazil nuts and heat until the sugar caramelizes, shaking the pan occasionally to ensure even cooking.

Remove the cling film from the cooked sponge pudding and leave to rest for 1 minute before turning out onto a warm plate.

When the caramel reaches a deep, rich amber colour, remove from the heat and pour onto a cold non-stick baking sheet. Wait for a minute or so and then shatter with a rolling pin.

Pour the custard into a jug and pour some over the pudding. Decorate with the nut brittle and serve with the rest of the custard so that people can help themselves.

Brian Turner
POACHED FIGS WITH VANILLA YOGHURT

Choose unbruised fruit, and I don't think it matters whether they are black or white – or purple or brown or green. The colour varies according to where they are from, though the purple ones tend to be most common.

Serves 2

1 miniature bottle port (about 50 ml (2 fl oz) in total)
finely grated rind and juice 1 orange
1 vanilla pod, split in half and seeds scraped out
1 tbsp light muscovado sugar
2 ripe firm figs
75 g (3 oz) Greek yoghurt
1–2 tsp icing sugar

Place the port in a pan with the orange rind and juice, scraped-out vanilla pod and muscovado sugar. Bring to a simmer and allow to reduce for a couple of minutes.

Cut the figs into quarters and carefully add to the pan. Poach for 3–4 minutes until tender, spooning over the port liquid occasionally to ensure the figs cook evenly.

Meanwhile, place the yoghurt in a bowl and beat in the vanilla seeds and icing sugar to taste.

Spoon the poached figs into warmed wide-rimmed bowls and continue to reduce the remaining poaching liquid for another couple of minutes until slightly sticky. Drizzle over the figs and add a dollop of the vanilla yoghurt to the side to serve.

Gino D'Acampo
SPICED MANGO WITH LIME-SCENTED CREAM

The flavour of mango is brought alive with a touch of chilli in this unusual dessert. It would also be delicious cooked in foil parcels over gentle coals at the end of a barbecue.

Serves 2

1 large ripe mango
1 tbsp clear honey
juice 1 lime
good pinch dried crushed chilli flakes
1 tbsp light muscovado sugar

FOR THE LIME-SCENTED CREAM
100 ml (3½ fl oz) double cream
4 fresh mint leaves, shredded
finely grated rind of 1 lime
about 1 tbsp sifted icing sugar

Preheat the oven to 200°C/400°F/Gas 6. Peel the mango and cut the flesh away from the stone, then cut into chunks. Spread out on a non-stick baking sheet and drizzle over the honey and lime juice. Scatter the crushed chillies and muscovado sugar on top and bake for 5 minutes until the sugar has melted and begun to caramelize.

Meanwhile, make the lime-scented cream. Whip the cream until soft peaks have formed. Shred the mint and fold into the cream with the lime rind and enough icing sugar to sweeten.

Divide the spiced mango between plates and add a good dollop of the lime cream to serve.

the ten-minute cookbook

Antony Worrall Thompson
POACHED PEACHES WITH SABAYON

Choose the ripest peaches for this exquisite dessert and they will poach in no time at all. If you like, reduce the poaching liquid and drizzle round the peaches before adding the sabayon.

Serves 2

25 g (1 oz) caster sugar
300 ml (½ pint) Muscat wine
2 ripe peaches

FOR THE SABAYON
3 egg yolks
25 g (1 oz) caster sugar
2 tbsp Muscat wine
½ vanilla pod, split in half and seeds
  scraped out

Heat the sugar and Muscat wine in a small pan until the sugar has dissolved. Cut the peaches in half and remove the stone, then add to the pan, ensuring they are completely covered in the liquid. Poach for 6–8 minutes until tender, basting occasionally as the liquid reduces.

Meanwhile, make the sabayon. Place the egg yolks, sugar, wine and vanilla seeds in a heatproof bowl set over a pan of simmering water. Using a large balloon whisk, beat for 6–8 minutes until the sabayon becomes pale and thickened and leaves a trail when you lift the whisk.

Transfer the peaches to warmed wide-rimmed bowls with a slotted spoon and ladle over the sabayon to serve.

Tony Tobin
RASPBERRY FRANGIPANE

This is an incredibly easy pudding, best made in the summer when British raspberries are at their best. Or use blackberries, blueberries or stoned cherries instead – whatever's in season.

Serves 2

100 g (4 oz) macadamia nuts
50 g (2 oz) butter, plus extra
  for greasing
2 tbsp caster sugar
2 tbsp self raising flour
1 egg
25 g (1 oz) raspberries
icing sugar, to dust
crème fraiche, to serve

Preheat the oven to 200°C/400°F/Gas 6. Place the macadamia nuts in a mini food processor and grind down.

Place the butter and sugar in a food processor and whiz until well creamed together. Add the ground macadamias, flour and egg. Continue to blend until you have a smooth batter.

Divide the raspberries between two buttered blini pans and pour over the batter. Place on the top shelf in the oven and bake for 8 minutes or until well risen and golden brown.

Turn the raspberry frangipanes out onto plates, add a light dusting of icing sugar and serve at once with a quenelle of crème fraiche on the side.

James Tanner
PANETTONE BREAD AND BUTTER PUDDING

This is a quick version of a classic pudding that's just perfect when you are tired and jaded.
I make this at Christmas, when there always seems to be leftover panettone about. ◄

Serves 2

300 ml (½ pint) milk
4 egg yolks
2 tbsp caster sugar
few drops vanilla extract
50 g (2 oz) unsalted butter
175 g (6 oz) piece panettone,
    cut into triangles
icing sugar, to dust

Preheat the oven to 220°C/425°F/Gas 7 and heat a large frying pan. Scald the milk in a small pan until almost boiling.

Meanwhile, whisk the egg yolks, sugar and vanilla extract in a large bowl, then gradually whisk this mixture into the scalded milk in the pan. Cook for a few minutes until the mixture begins to thicken and coat the back of a wooden spoon.

Melt half the butter in the frying pan and quickly fry half the panettone triangles until lightly golden. Arrange in an overlapping layer in a small ovenproof dish and repeat with the rest of the butter and panettone. Pour over the custard and press down gently with a fish slice. Place on a baking sheet and bake in the oven for 4–5 minutes until the custard is almost but not quite set.

Remove the pudding from the oven, dust with icing sugar and flash with a blowtorch until lightly caramelized. Serve at once.

James Martin
STICKY TOFFEE PUDDING

The king of puddings. It is not very slimming, mind you, but sometimes you just want to forget about diets and enjoy yourself. The dates are my secret key ingredient and give a deep toffee-like flavour to the pudding.

Serves 2

50 g (2 oz) unsalted butter, plus extra
    for greasing
50 g (2 oz) light muscovado sugar
1 egg
25 g (1 oz) dates, stoned and chopped
50 g (2 oz) self-raising flour
pinch baking powder

FOR THE TOFFEE SAUCE
200 ml (7 fl oz) double cream
50 g (2 oz) light muscovado sugar
25 g (1 oz) unsalted butter

Cream the butter and sugar in a food processor. Add the egg, dates, flour and baking powder and pulse until smooth.

Grease a microwavable pudding dish that is about 23 x 15 cm (9 x 6 in) across and 2.5 cm (1 in) deep with butter. Using a spatula, fill with the sponge mixture. Cover with cling film and pierce the top a couple of times with a sharp knife. Cook in the microwave on high for 4 minutes.

To make the toffee sauce, place the cream, sugar and butter in a small pan and heat gently for a few minutes until smooth.

Remove the pudding from the microwave and turn out onto a plate. Pour over the toffee sauce and serve at once.

Tony Tobin
WINTER BERRY SPONGE WITH CUSTARD

This microwaved version of a steamed pudding is nursery food at its best. It has a lovely dense, moist texture. Be warned – there will be requests for second helpings.

Serves 2

100 g (4 oz) frozen mixed berries
150 g (5 oz) caster sugar
100 g (4 oz) self-raising flour
1 tsp baking powder
100 g (4 oz) butter, plus extra
    for greasing
3 large eggs
1 vanilla pod, split in half and
    seeds scraped out
2 tbsp red wine

FOR THE CUSTARD
50 ml (2 fl oz) milk
100 ml (3½ fl oz) double cream
1 vanilla pod, split in half and
    seeds scraped out
3 large egg yolks
50 g (2 oz) caster sugar

Defrost the berries in the microwave, then drain and reserve the juice. Place the berries in a food processor with 100 g (4 oz) of the sugar, the flour, baking powder, butter, eggs and vanilla seeds. Blend until well combined.

Butter a 1.2 litre (2 pint) microwavable pudding basin and spoon in the sponge mixture – it should be no more than two-thirds full to give the pudding room to rise. Cover with cling film, pierce the top once or twice with a sharp knife and then cook on high for 8 minutes until well risen and cooked through.

Meanwhile, make the custard. Place the milk, cream and vanilla seeds and pod in a small pan and bring to a simmering point, then set aside to infuse.

Whisk the egg yolks and sugar in a large bowl until soft and fluffy. Remove the vanilla pod from the heated milk mixture and discard, then gradually add the milk to the whisked egg yolks and sugar. Pour back into a clean pan and cook gently for about 5 minutes until the custard coats the back of a wooden spoon, stirring regularly.

To make the fruit syrup, place the reserved berry juice – you should have about four tablespoons in total – in a small pan with the remaining sugar and the red wine. Bring to the boil and boil fast for 2 minutes until slightly reduced and thickened, stirring occasionally.

Remove the winter berry sponge from the microwave and turn out onto a plate. Pour over the fruit syrup and allow it to soak in, and serve with a jug of the custard to allow people to help themselves.

James Martin
UPSIDE-DOWN PINEAPPLE SPONGE WITH CARAMEL SAUCE

I've always loved baking – I was brought up in the country and had a lovely Gran who used to let me 'help' her in the kitchen from when I was very young. This recipe was a real experiment and I wasn't sure it was going to work, but the result was a knockout.

Serves 2

100 g (4 oz) unsalted butter, softened, plus extra for greasing
100 g (4 oz) caster sugar
1 egg
100 g (4 oz) self-raising flour
1 tbsp clear honey
4 slices pineapple, drained if from a can

FOR THE CARAMEL SAUCE
50 g (2 oz) unsalted butter
50 g (2 oz) caster sugar
2 tbsp clear honey

Cream the butter and sugar together in a large bowl until pale and fluffy. Beat in the egg and then fold in the flour.

Grease a 1.2 litre (2 pint) microwavable pudding basin with butter and drizzle with the honey. Arrange the pineapple slices round the inside of the bowl and spoon in the sponge mixture. Cover with cling film, pierce once or twice with a fork and microwave on high for 6 minutes until well risen and lightly golden.

Meanwhile, make the caramel sauce. Melt the butter in a pan and add the sugar and honey. Heat gently for 3–4 minutes until slightly reduced and thickened.

Remove the pineapple sponge from the microwave and turn out onto a plate. Drizzle over the caramel sauce and serve at once.

Paul Rankin
RHUBARB AND STEM GINGER CRUMBLE

A little indulgence is a wonderful thing and it doesn't come much better than this. The ultimate comforting dessert made from start to finish in under ten minutes – not bad, if I say so myself …

Serves 2

2 rhubarb stalks, trimmed and finely chopped
50 g (2 oz) caster sugar
4 knobs crystallized stem ginger, drained and finely chopped
2 tsp cornflour
50 g (2 oz) Hobnob biscuits
25 g (1 oz) butter, chilled and diced
25 g (1 oz) macadamia nuts
2 scoops vanilla ice cream, to serve

Preheat the oven to 200°C/400°F/Gas 6. Place the rhubarb, sugar, ginger and cornflour in a microwavable bowl. Stir to combine and cover with cling film. Microwave on high for 3 minutes until the rhubarb is cooked through but still holding its shape.

Meanwhile, place the biscuits, butter and macadamia nuts in a food processor and whiz until just broken down – it's important the mix has a coarse texture. Set aside.

Divide the cooked rhubarb mixture between two 200 ml (7 fl oz) ramekins and sprinkle the crumble mixture on top. Arrange on a baking sheet and bake for about 5 minutes until the topping is crisp and golden brown.

Place the ramekins on plates and add a scoop of ice cream on top to serve.

Ross Burden
ICE CREAM TOWER WAFFLES WITH PECAN PRALINE AND TOFFEE SAUCE

This recipe would also work well with ready-made Scotch pancakes or split croissants.

Serves 2

sunflower oil, for greasing
2 Belgian waffles
4–6 small scoops vanilla ice cream

FOR THE TOFFEE SAUCE
4 tbsp maple syrup
25 g (1 oz) butter
2 tbsp double cream

FOR THE PECAN PRALINE
100 g (4 oz) caster sugar
50 g (2 oz) toasted pecan nuts

Preheat the oven to 220°C/425°F/Gas 7. Lightly oil two baking sheets.

To make the toffee sauce, place the maple syrup, butter and cream in a pan and heat gently for 2–3 minutes until smooth. Set aside to cool.

To make the pecan praline, place the sugar in a very clean, heavy-based pan and heat gently until it has dissolved. Then bring to the boil and boil fast for a few minutes until the resulting syrup begins to turn pale brown, gently swirling the pan to ensure even cooking.

When the caramel is a rich golden brown colour, dip the base of the pan into a sink of cool water to prevent further cooking. Add the toasted pecan nuts, shaking the pan to coat evenly. Pour the pecan caramel mixture onto one of the oiled baking sheets, leaving some of the caramel behind in the pan.

To make the spun sugar, take a clean, small metal spoon and a knife-sharpening steel, and dip the spoon into the remaining caramel. Move the spoon up and down the steel, pulling the sugar with your fingers until a candy-floss texture is achieved. Carefully transfer to the remaining oiled baking sheet and repeat with another spoonful.

Place the waffles on another baking sheet and cook for 3 minutes or until completely heated through.

Meanwhile, break the set pecan praline into small pieces with a rolling pin.

Place the hot waffles on warmed plates and top with the scoops of ice cream. Sprinkle over the pecan praline and drizzle the toffee sauce on top. Place some of the spun sugar on the top of each dessert in a tall pile and serve at once.

James Martin
UPSIDE-DOWN APRICOT PANCAKES

This dessert makes great use of the store cupboard. It's perfect for when you fancy something sweet but don't have much in the house. Use canned pears, peaches or cherries with excellent results.

Serves 2

100 g (4 oz) caster sugar
50 g (2 oz) plain flour
50 g (2 oz) butter
1 egg
1 vanilla pod, split in half and
  seeds scraped out
400 g (14 oz) can apricot halves
  in syrup, drained
vanilla ice cream, to serve

Preheat the oven to 200°C/400°F/Gas 6. Heat 50 g (2 oz) of the sugar in an ovenproof sauté pan until it begins to dissolve and caramelize, swirling the pan occasionally to ensure it cooks evenly.

Meanwhile, place the flour in a food processor with the remaining sugar, butter, egg and vanilla seeds. Blend to a smooth batter.

Arrange the apricot halves, cut-side up, in the caramel in the bottom of the pan. Take the pan off the heat, pour over the batter, transfer to the oven and bake for about 8 minutes until well risen and golden brown.

Invert the pancake onto a flat plate and rearrange the apricots as necessary. Slice and serve on warmed plates with a scoop of ice cream.

Ross Burden
PANCAKES WITH LEMON SYRUP

This is a variation on an all-time classic – crêpes Suzettes. Brilliant for last-minute entertaining as these are ingredients most of us have to hand.

Serves 2

50 g (2 oz) plain flour
pinch salt
1 egg
150 ml (¼ pint) milk
sunflower oil, for cooking
50 g (2 oz) butter
50 g (2 oz) caster sugar
finely grated rind and juice 2 lemons
Greek yoghurt, to serve
fresh mint sprigs, to decorate (optional)

Heat a heavy-based frying pan. Sift the flour and salt into a bowl and make a well in the centre. Add the egg and whisk vigorously with a balloon whisk. Gradually beat in the milk, drawing in the flour from the sides to make a smooth batter.

Put a little oil in the hot frying pan. Pour in just enough batter to thinly coat the base. Cook over a medium to high heat for about 1 minute until golden brown. Turn or toss and cook on the other side for another 30 seconds or so – you'll need four in total. When the pancakes are cooked, fold each one into a triangle shape by folding in half and then in half again.

Meanwhile, heat the butter and sugar in a separate heavy-based pan until thick and syrupy. Add the lemon rind and juice and allow to warm through. Add the pancake triangles to the pan and spoon over the lemon syrup to coat evenly.

Arrange the pancakes with the lemon syrup on warmed plates and add a dollop of Greek yoghurt. Decorate with mint sprigs, if liked, to serve.

Phil Vickery
PAIN PERDU WITH CARAMELIZED PEACH SAUCE

Called 'perdu' (lost) because the stale bread would otherwise be thrown away.

Serves 2

2 eggs
2 tbsp milk
2 tbsp double cream
1 tbsp caster sugar
4 slices brioche (1 day old is best)
25 g (1 oz) butter

FOR THE CARAMELIZED PEACH SAUCE

75 g (3 oz) caster sugar
200 g (7 oz) can peach slices in natural juice

Heat a large sauté pan. Break the eggs into a shallow dish with the milk, cream and sugar. Whisk until well combined. Using a cookie cutter, stamp out circles from the slices of brioche and soak each one in the egg mixture. Melt the butter in the heated sauté pan. Once it starts foaming, add the soaked brioche and cook for 3–4 minutes until golden brown, turning once.

Meanwhile, make the peach sauce. Melt the sugar over a gentle heat in a heavy-based pan, swirling the pan occasionally so it cooks evenly. Increase the heat under the melted sugar and bring to the boil, then boil fast until the sugar syrup begins to caramelize. Stir four tablespoons of the juice from the peaches into the caramel to prevent it cooking any further. Pour the caramel into a food processor and add the peach slices. Blend to a smooth sauce, adding a little more peach juice if necessary.

Arrange the pain perdu on warmed plates and spoon over the sauce to serve.

Nick Nairn
BANANA SOUFFLÉ WITH WALNUT BUTTERSCOTCH

The secret to a good soufflé is to butter the moulds well and not to over-whisk the egg whites. The ready-made custard saves time and makes these beauties achievable in less than ten minutes.

Serves 2

knob butter
2 egg whites
1 tsp fresh lemon juice
1 ripe banana
1 egg yolk
2 tbsp ready-made custard
icing sugar, to dust

FOR THE WALNUT BUTTERSCOTCH

25 g (1 oz) walnut halves
50 g (2 oz) Demerara sugar
25 g (1 oz) butter
85 ml (3 fl oz) double cream
1 vanilla pod, split in half and seeds scraped out

Preheat the oven to 200°C/400°F/Gas 6. Roast the walnuts for the sauce in a small baking tin for about 5 minutes until lightly toasted. Grease two 120 ml (4 fl oz) ramekins with butter. Place the egg whites and lemon juice in a large bowl and whisk to soft peaks.

Mash the banana in a separate bowl and mix in the egg yolk and custard until well combined. Using a large metal spoon, carefully fold in the egg whites. Divide the soufflé mixture between the ramekins and place on the top shelf in the oven for 8 minutes until well risen and lightly golden.

Meanwhile, make the walnut butterscotch. Place the sugar in a heavy-based pan with the butter, cream and vanilla seeds. Heat gently until the sugar has dissolved, stirring occasionally. Increase the heat and cook for another couple of minutes until you have a thick, smooth sauce. Finely chop the roasted walnuts and stir them in at the end. Keep warm.

Remove the soufflés from the oven and dust with icing sugar. Arrange on plates with individual jugs of the walnut butterscotch to serve.

hot desserts

147

cold desserts

Antony Worrall Thompson
AMARETTI CHEESECAKE WITH CARAMELIZED WALNUTS

A dessert with an unusual flavour combination, which looks spectacular but involves little effort – what could be better?

Serves 2

150 ml (¼ pint) double cream
4 tbsp ricotta cheese
finely grated rind of 1 lemon
few drops vanilla extract
100 ml (3½ fl oz) dry white wine
75 g (3 oz) amaretti biscuits
2 ripe figs
icing sugar, to dust

FOR THE CARAMELIZED WALNUTS

50 g (2 oz) caster sugar
50 g (2 oz) walnut halves

To make the caramelized walnuts, place the caster sugar in a heavy-based frying pan and heat until the sugar dissolves, without stirring. Increase the heat and cook for another few minutes until a light caramel colour is achieved. Add the walnuts, shaking the pan to coat evenly, then spoon the walnuts onto a sheet of non-stick parchment paper and leave to cool and harden.

Meanwhile, place the cream in a large bowl and whisk until soft peaks have formed. Fold in the ricotta, lemon rind and vanilla extract until well combined.

Take two 10 cm (4 in) metal cooking rings and put one on each plate. Pour the wine into a small bowl. Quickly dip the amaretti biscuits in the wine, then arrange them in the bottom of the cooking rings, slightly crushing to fit.

Spoon half of the cream mixture over the two rings and level it with the back of a spoon. Add another layer of the dampened, lightly crushed amaretti biscuits, and cover with the rest of the cream mixture, smoothing across the top with a palette knife.

Cut each fig into thin slices and arrange in a fan shape over each cheesecake, covering the cream completely. Dust liberally with icing sugar and flash with a blowtorch until lightly caramelized. Briefly heat the sides of the cooking rings with a blowtorch to remove them easily. Decorate each plate with the caramelized walnuts to serve.

cold desserts

Paul Rankin
LEMON CURD CHEESECAKE

This dessert is perfect if you're short on time but searching for the wow factor. It looks as if you've been slaving in the kitchen, but only minutes before you present it in all its glory it was just a bought flan case.

Serves 4–6

2 tbsp lemon curd
1 tbsp caster sugar
finely grated rind and juice 1 lemon
250 g (9 oz) flan sponge case
75 g (3 oz) redcurrants
50 g (2 oz) bar white chocolate

FOR THE FILLING
100 g (4 oz) mascarpone cheese
1 tbsp icing sugar, plus extra
   for dusting
finely grated rind and juice ½ lemon
120 ml (4fl oz) double cream
2 tbsp lemon curd

To make a lemon glaze, heat the lemon curd and caster sugar with the lemon rind and juice in a small pan for 2–3 minutes until the sugar has dissolved, stirring occasionally.

Place the flan case on a flat plate and drizzle over the lemon glaze in an even layer. Set aside to allow the lemon to penetrate the sponge.

Meanwhile, prepare the filling. Place the mascarpone in a bowl with the icing sugar, lemon rind and juice and double cream. Whisk until you have achieved soft peaks, then fold in the lemon curd for a ripple effect.

Pile the filling into the flan case. Using a palette knife, smooth the top. Scatter over the redcurrants and pare shavings of the white chocolate on top. Finally add a light dusting of icing sugar and chill until ready to serve.

" I've curd you're my number one flan ,

Nick Nairn
INSTANT TIRAMISU

There are lots of tiramisus doing the rounds at the moment – this is my version!

Serves 2

250 g (9 oz) curd or cream cheese
2 tbsp double cream
1 vanilla pod, split in half and seeds
    scraped out
4 tbsp strong black coffee
25 g (3 oz) caster sugar
50 g (4 oz) sponge fingers, snapped
    in half
50 g (4 oz) mixed blueberries
    and raspberries
1 miniature Grand Marnier (about
    50 ml (2 fl oz) in total)
25 g (1 oz) plain chocolate,
    finely grated

Whisk the curd cheese, double cream and vanilla seeds in a large bowl until thickened.

Mix the coffee and caster sugar in a shallow dish. Dip in half of the sponge fingers, then arrange in the base of individual dessert glasses.

Scatter over the blueberries and raspberries and drizzle half of the Grand Marnier on top, then cover with the creamy vanilla mixture. Scatter over half of the grated chocolate.

Repeat the layers until all the ingredients have been used up, finishing with a layer of grated chocolate. Serve at once.

Phil Vickery
CRÈME BRÛLÉE

It's always nice to be able to produce a quick and simple version of a classic. I use a blowtorch at home to caramelize the top of puddings. Easy-to-use models are available in kitchen shops.

Serves 2

150 ml (¼ pint) condensed milk
    (from a can)
50 ml (2 fl oz) milk
2 egg yolks
icing sugar, to dust

Preheat the oven to 220°C/425°F/Gas 7. Place the condensed milk in a small pan with the milk and egg yolks. Cook over a gentle heat for 2–3 minutes until the mixture coats the back of a wooden spoon, stirring constantly.

Divide the mixture between two 100 ml (3½ fl oz) ramekins and place on a baking sheet. Put on the top shelf of the oven for 5–6 minutes until just set.

Sit each ramekin in a bowl of ice cubes so that it cools down as quickly as possible. Dust the top liberally with icing sugar and then flash each one with a blowtorch until the tops are caramelized. Set on plates and serve at once.

❝Dessert island dishes❞

James Tanner
MANGO MOUSSE IN BRANDY SNAPS

This clever little dessert requires no cooking at all. For those with a sweeter tooth, drizzle a little of the syrup of the stem ginger over the mango mousse to serve.

Serves 2

1 small ripe mango
juice 1 lime
4 tbsp double cream
1 knob crystallized stem ginger, finely chopped, plus 1 tbsp ginger syrup
4 fresh mint leaves, shredded, plus fresh mint sprigs, to decorate
2 brandy-snap baskets

Peel the mango and cut away the flesh, discarding the stone. Place in a mini blender with the lime juice and blitz to a smooth purée.

Whip the cream in a bowl until soft peaks have formed. Fold in four tablespoons of the mango purée with the stem ginger, ginger syrup and shredded mint until well combined.

Spoon the mango mousse into the brandy-snap baskets set on plates and decorate with the mint sprigs. Drizzle the remaining mango purée round the edges of the plates, loosening it with a little water if necessary. Serve at once.

Ross Burden
CHOCOLATE ORANGE MOUSSE

A little indulgence is a wonderful thing and good quality chocolate makes all the difference in this recipe, so try to get chocolate with a minimum of 70 per cent cocoa solids.

Serves 2

50 g (2 oz) plain chocolate, broken into squares
1 orange
200 ml (7 fl oz) double cream, well chilled
2 tbsp sifted icing sugar, plus extra for dusting
cocoa powder, for dusting

Melt the chocolate in the microwave on high for 2 minutes or set over a pan of simmering water for 3 minutes. As soon as it has melted, transfer to a cold bowl with a spatula to help it cool down as quickly as possible.

Finely grate the rind from the orange and set aside. Using a very sharp knife, remove any remaining skin and all the white pith, then carefully cut into segments and reserve to decorate.

Whip the cream with the icing sugar and orange rind in a large bowl until soft peaks have formed. When the melted chocolate has cooled sufficiently, fold it into the cream mixture to achieve a rippled marble effect.

Set a 10 cm (4 in) metal cooking ring on each plate and fill with the chocolate orange mousse. Quickly and carefully, use a blowtorch to warm each ring before removing it again. Decorate the plates with the orange segments and add a light dusting of the icing sugar and cocoa powder to serve.

cold desserts

153

James Martin
LEMON STRAWBERRY WAFER STACKS WITH RASPBERRY COULIS

Sugar work has become my trademark on Ready Steady Cook, but I may have to acquire another one. I used to win with it every time but now the audience have become more critical, and however impressive the spun sugar it doesn't always guarantee the vote.

Serves 2

75 g (3 oz) caster sugar
4 tbsp mascarpone cheese
100 ml (3 fl oz) double cream
1 tsp sifted icing sugar, plus extra
    for dusting
1 tbsp lemon curd
6 round thin shortbread biscuits (each
    about 5–7.5 cm (2–3 in) in diameter)
12 evenly sized small strawberries
    (about 150 g (5 oz) in weight)

FOR THE RASPBERRY COULIS
100 g (4 oz) raspberries
juice 1 lime
2 tsp sifted icing sugar

Place the sugar in a very clean, heavy-based pan and heat gently until it has dissolved. Then bring to the boil and boil fast for a few minutes until the resulting syrup begins to turn pale brown, gently swirling the pan to ensure even cooking.

Meanwhile, place the mascarpone in a bowl with the cream, icing sugar and lemon curd. Mix until well combined. Place one shortbread biscuit on each plate and divide half of the mascarpone mixture between them.

Remove the stalks from the strawberries and cut them in half. Stand up six of the strawberry halves in the mascarpone mixture on each shortbread, cut-side facing out. Cover with another shortbread biscuit and repeat the mascarpone and strawberry layer. Finish each stack with the two remaining biscuits and dust with icing sugar.

Heat a flat metal skewer on an open flame and carefully mark the tops of the stacks, reheating the skewer as necessary.

To make the raspberry coulis, place the raspberries, lime juice and icing sugar in a mini food processor and blend until smooth. Pass through a sieve into a bowl and then pour into a jug. Drizzle around each strawberry stack.

When the caramel is a rich golden-brown colour, dip the base of the pan into a sink of cold water to prevent further cooking. To make the spun sugar, take a clean, small metal spoon and a knife-sharpening steel, and dip the spoon into the caramel. Move the spoon up and down the steel, pulling the sugar with your fingers until a candy-floss texture is achieved. Pile some of the spun sugar on top and serve at once.

Tony Tobin
BLACK FOREST LAYER WITH WHITE CHOCOLATE SAUCE

A classic dessert with a *Ready Steady Cook* accent. Impressive, decadent and incredibly easy to make. ▶

Serves 2

200 ml (7 fl oz) double cream
4 tbsp Tia Maria
2 tbsp sifted icing sugar
2 large chocolate muffins
12 cherries preserved in
    brandy, drained
cocoa powder, to dust

FOR THE WHITE CHOCOLATE SAUCE

200 ml (7 fl oz) double cream
100 g (4 oz) white chocolate, broken
    in pieces

To make the white chocolate sauce, place the cream in a small pan and bring to scalding point (almost but not quite to the boil). Remove from the heat, stir in the white chocolate and allow to melt. Leave to cool a little.

Place the cream in a large bowl with the Tia Maria and icing sugar and whisk until soft peaks have formed. Cut each muffin horizontally into three even slices and use half to fill the bottom of two 10 cm (4 in) metal cooking rings, breaking up as necessary. Cover with half of the flavoured cream and scatter the cherries on top. Add another layer of the muffin to enclose the cherries and cream completely. Spoon the rest of the flavoured cream on top and spread evenly with a palette knife. Dust liberally with the cocoa powder and, using a blowtorch briefly round the sides to help release them, carefully remove the cooking rings. Drizzle round the cooled white chocolate sauce and serve at once.

Brian Turner
BANANA AND CHOCOLATE TRIFLE

Bananas and chocolate are a classic combination, and with a measure of Baileys Irish Cream this is a dessert to die for.

Serves 2

100 g (4 oz) ready-made chocolate
    slab cake
1 large banana
1 miniature Baileys Irish Cream
    (about 50 ml (2 fl oz) in total)
120 ml (4 fl oz) double cream
cocoa powder, to dust

FOR THE PECAN BRITTLE

sunflower oil, for greasing
50 g (2 oz) caster sugar
25 g (1 oz) toasted pecan nuts,
    roughly chopped

To make the pecan brittle, lightly oil a baking sheet, then place the sugar in a very clean, heavy-based pan and heat gently until it has dissolved. Bring to the boil and boil fast for a few minutes until the resulting syrup begins to turn pale brown, gently swirling the pan to ensure even cooking. When the caramel is a rich golden-brown, dip the base of the pan into a sink of cold water to prevent further cooking. Add the toasted pecan nuts, shaking the pan to coat evenly. Pour onto the oiled baking sheet and leave to set.

Meanwhile, cut the chocolate cake into small pieces and use about half to line two individual glass dishes. Slice the banana and divide between the dishes. Sprinkle over half of the Baileys Irish Cream, then arrange the remaining cake on top in an even layer. Whip the cream and the remaining Baileys in a bowl until soft peaks have formed. Swirl over the chocolate cake layer to cover completely. Break the pecan brittle into small pieces with a rolling pin and scatter on top. Add a light dusting of cocoa powder and serve at once.

Lesley Waters
PEACH MELBA KNICKERBOCKER GLORY

A glorious finale to any meal, and the real beauty of these is that they are assembled in minutes.

Serves 2

1 tbsp flaked almonds
2 ready-made meringue nests
1 ripe peach or nectarine, halved, stone
   removed and sliced
100 g (4 oz) raspberries
4 scoops vanilla ice cream
4 biscuit curls or 'cigars'

FOR THE FUDGE SAUCE
4 tbsp double cream
50 g (2 oz) butter
50 g (2 oz) light muscovado sugar
juice ½ orange

First make the fudge sauce. Place the cream in a small pan with the butter, sugar and orange juice. Heat gently until the sugar dissolves, then simmer for 4–5 minutes until slightly reduced and fudge-like. Remove from the heat and allow to cool a little.

Toast the almond flakes in a dry frying pan, tossing occasionally to ensure they cook evenly. Tip out onto a plate to cool.

Lightly crush the meringue nests and arrange in the base of two tall glasses. Scatter over the peach or nectarine with half of the raspberries, and top each one with two scoops of the ice cream. Top with the remaining raspberries.

Drizzle the fudge sauce generously into each glass. Sprinkle over the toasted nuts and decorate with the biscuits to serve.

' Almond top of the world with knickerbocker glory '

Gino D'Acampo
POACHED PLUMS WITH CHOCOLATE CREAM

I didn't add any sugar to the liquid I poached the plums in because the chocolate cream is sweet enough. This would also be delicious with some biscotti for dipping into the cream.

Serves 2

3 ripe small plums, halved and
    stones removed
120 ml (4 fl oz) red wine
juice 1 lemon

FOR THE CHOCOLATE CREAM
100 g (4 oz) plain chocolate
250 g (9 oz) carton mascarpone cheese
about 2 tbsp sifted icing sugar

Place the plums in a pan with the red wine and lemon juice. Bring to the boil, then reduce the heat and simmer for 4–5 minutes until the plums are tender.

Meanwhile, melt the chocolate in the microwave or in a heatproof bowl set over a pan of simmering water. Quickly beat in the mascarpone and enough icing sugar to taste.

Drain the plums and place in the freezer for a couple of minutes to cool down quickly.

Place a 7.5 cm (3 in) metal cooking ring in the centre of each plate and fill with the chocolate cream. Heat the sides with a mini-blowtorch and carefully remove the rings. Arrange the cooled plums round the chocolate and serve at once.

Phil Vickery
FRUITS OF THE FOREST SPONGE

This dessert is a favourite in my house. The kids love getting involved and have great fun lining the cooking rings. If it's for adults only, add a splash of cassis or your favourite liqueur to the ricotta mixture.

Serves 2

300 g (11 oz) can forest fruits in
    light syrup
12 sponge fingers
175 g (6 oz) ricotta cheese
100 ml (3½ fl oz) double cream
4 tbsp Greek yoghurt
¼ lemon, pips removed
50 g (2 oz) bar plain chocolate
icing sugar, to dust

Drain the juice from the can of fruit into a shallow dish, reserving the fruit. Dip the sponge fingers briefly into the juice and use them to line two 10 cm (4 in) metal cooking rings set on plates, standing them up so the tops protrude.

Place the ricotta cheese in a bowl with the cream, yoghurt and a squeeze of the lemon juice. Add four tablespoons of the drained fruit juice. Whip to form soft peaks, then use to fill the sponge-lined rings, almost but not quite to the top. Spoon a couple of tablespoons of the reserved forest fruits on top of the ricotta mixture so they come to the top of the sponge fingers. Grate over the chocolate.

Blitz the remaining juice and fruit in a mini food processor with a squeeze of lemon juice. Pass through a fine sieve into a jug and then drizzle round the plate. Carefully remove the cooking rings and dust the sponges with a little icing sugar to serve.

drinks

Antony Worrall Thompson
MINT AND GINGER-INFUSED TEA

This tea has incredible natural healing properties and is just the thing if you are feeling under the weather with a cold or flu.

Serves 2

600 ml (1 pint) boiling water
5 cm (2 in) piece root ginger
good handful fresh mint leaves
2 tbsp clear honey

Pour a little of the boiling water into the teapot and set aside for a couple of minutes to warm through.

Thinly slice the ginger. Pour out the water from the teapot and add the ginger, mint and honey with the rest of the boiling water, stirring with a long spoon until the honey has dissolved. Set aside for 3–4 minutes to allow all the ingredients to infuse, then pour into cups while still hot to serve.

Tony Tobin
LYCHEE AND RASPBERRY LASSI

This would be a fantastic finale to any meal. Use a drained can of lychees in syrup if you have difficulty finding fresh ones.

Serves 2

20 ripe lychees
2 tbsp clear honey
1 vanilla pod, split in half and seeds scraped out
4 tbsp Greek yoghurt
good handful ice cubes
50 g (2 oz) raspberries
juice 1 lime

Peel the lychees and remove the stones, then place in a liquidizer with the honey, vanilla seeds, Greek yoghurt and ice. Blend until smooth and pour into two tall glasses.

Place the raspberries and lime juice in a small bowl and mash together with a fork. Divide between the two glasses and stir once or twice to create a ripple effect. Serve at once.

Brian Turner
SCENTED GRAPEFRUIT JUICE

A refreshing drink that would be a perfect start to the day. It's a light breakfast-in-a-glass, and much tastier than anything you can buy. ◀

Serves 2

1 ripe grapefruit
1 lime
6 fresh mint leaves
handful ice cubes
1–2 tbsp clear honey

Cut the grapefruit and lime in half and squeeze the juice into a liquidizer. Add the mint, ice and one tablespoon of the honey. Whiz until well combined, then taste and add a little more honey if you think it needs it.

Pour the scented grapefruit juice into glasses to serve.

Paul Rankin
MANGO AND COCONUT SPLASH

For a variation, try replacing the mango with a chopped banana or some chopped pawpaw with twice the lime juice.

Serves 2

1 ripe firm mango
2 tbsp clear honey
100 ml (4 fl oz) Greek yoghurt
200 ml (7fl oz) coconut milk
juice 1 lime
handful ice cubes

Peel the mango, cut away all the flesh from the stone and place in a liquidizer. Add the honey with the yoghurt, coconut milk and lime juice. Tip in the ice cubes with 100 ml (3½ fl oz) of water and blend to a purée.

Pour the drink into tall glasses and serve at once.

Phil Vickery
MELON AND ORANGE SMOOTHIE

Smoothies are now big business and it's easy to spend £3 or £4 on one when you're out and about, but they are very simple to make yourself when you're at home.

Serves 2

1 small ripe melon
4 oranges
2 limes
6 fresh basil leaves
200g (7 oz) carton Greek yoghurt
1–2 tbsp clear honey
good handful ice cubes

Cut the melon in half and scoop out the seeds. Using a spoon, scoop the flesh into a liquidizer. Cut the oranges and limes in half and squeeze in the juice. Add the basil with the yoghurt, one tablespoon of the honey and the ice cubes. Blend until smooth, then taste and add more honey if you think it needs it.

Pour into tall glasses and serve at once.

James Tanner
BANANA AND VANILLA BEAN SMOOTHIE

This is a favourite for adults and children alike. It's ideal for using up an overripe banana, and because of their natural sweetness you need only a little honey.

Serves 2

1 ripe banana
225 ml (8 fl oz) milk, well chilled
100 g (4 oz) Greek yoghurt
1 vanilla pod, split in half and seeds scraped out
1–2 tbsp clear honey
about 85 g (3 oz) ice cubes

Peel the banana and place in a liquidizer with the milk, yoghurt, vanilla seeds and one tablespoon of honey. Chuck in a handful of the ice cubes and blend until smooth. Taste and add a little more honey if necessary.

Fill tall glasses half-full with ice and then top up with the banana and vanilla bean smoothie. Serve at once.

non-alcoholic drinks

163

Lesley Waters
PINK PANTHER

Hold the redcurrant stalk and run the prongs of a fork through it to release the berries. ▶

Serves 2

100 g (4 oz) raspberries
squeeze lime juice
1 tbsp sifted icing sugar
50 g (2 oz) strawberries, hulled and halved if large
50 g (2 oz) redcurrants
2 tbsp Greek yoghurt
4 tbsp milk
good handful ice cubes

To make a raspberry coulis, blend 50 g (2 oz) of the raspberries with the lime juice and icing sugar in a mini food processor and then pass through a sieve.

Place the remaining raspberries, the strawberries, redcurrants, Greek yoghurt, milk and ice cubes in a liquidizer and blend until smooth.

Pour the berry mixture into tall glasses and then drizzle in the raspberry coulis to serve.

Lesley Waters
FRAPPACCINO

To add a caffeine hit to this, freeze your leftover coffee in ice cubes and use those.

Serves 2

2 tbsp cocoa powder
1 tbsp clear honey
4 tbsp double cream
4 large scoops vanilla ice cream
300ml (½ pint) milk
175 g (6 oz) ice cubes

Place the cocoa powder in a small pan with the honey and cream. Heat gently for a couple of minutes until a smooth chocolate sauce has formed, stirring occasionally.

Place the ice cream in a liquidizer with the milk and ice cubes. Blend until smooth, then pour in the chocolate sauce and blend again.

Pour the frappaccino into tall glasses and add a straw to each one to serve.

James Martin
FRESH COCONUT AND PEACH MILKSHAKE

This is a brilliant summertime drink, but you need good-quality vanilla ice cream made with real vanilla seeds for a truly spectacular result. It might be more expensive but it is worth every penny.

Serves 2

1 small coconut
2 firm, ripe peaches
4 scoops vanilla ice cream
4 tbsp Greek yoghurt
1 tsp caster sugar

Break open the coconut, reserving the milk. Break the coconut flesh into pieces and place in a liquidizer with the reserved coconut milk.

Drop the peaches into a pan of boiling water for 30 seconds, then slip off their skin and chop the flesh, discarding the stones. Add to the food processor with the ice cream, yoghurt and sugar. Blend until thick and smooth and then pour into tall glasses. Add straws to serve.

Phil Vickery
VIRGIN MARY

The secret of a good Virgin Mary is in the balance of the seasonings – experiment until you find the right combination for you.

Serves 2

400g (14 oz) can tomato juice
1 tbsp Worcestershire sauce
½ tsp Tabasco sauce
½ tsp salt
good pinch black pepper
juice 1 lime
1 tbsp chopped fresh coriander (optional)
about 175 g (6 oz) crushed ice
6 anchovy-stuffed green olives

Place the tomato juice in a large cocktail shaker with the Worcestershire sauce, Tabasco, salt, pepper and lime juice, and the coriander if liked. Fill up with ice and shake until very well chilled. Taste and adjust the seasoning as necessary.

Strain the Virgin Mary into tall, sturdy glasses, top with fresh ice and garnish each one with the olives. Add swizzle sticks to serve.

Antony Worrall Thompson
HOT CHOCOLATE WITH MARSHMALLOWS

There is something about chocolate that is addictive and this hot chocolate for grown-ups is no exception. I usually go for a rich Belgian chocolate, which is heavier in fats and cocoa solids than most British varieties. ◄

Serves 2

100 g (4 oz) plain chocolate, broken into squares
450 ml (¾ pint) milk
85 ml (3 fl oz) double cream
good handful tiny marshmallows

Melt the chocolate in a non-metallic bowl on high in the microwave for 2 minutes or set over a pan of simmering water for 3 minutes.

Place the milk and cream in a small heavy-based pan. Using a spatula, add the melted chocolate, stirring to combine. Heat gently for a few minutes, stirring continuously until piping hot but not boiling.

Pour the hot chocolate into large cappuccino cups or bowls and scatter the marshmallows on top to serve. Yummy!

Phil Vickery
HOT MARZIPAN MILKSHAKE

This is a brilliant way of using up a leftover piece of marzipan at Christmas or Easter.

Serves 2

2 vanilla pods
600 ml (1 pint) milk
100 g (4 oz) marzipan
4 scoops vanilla ice cream
cocoa powder, to dust

Cut each vanilla pod in half and, using a teaspoon, scrape out the seeds. Place the seeds in a pan with the milk and marzipan and cook for 2–3 minutes until heated through, stirring occasionally.

Transfer the marzipan mixture to a liquidizer and blend until smooth. Pour into tall glasses and top each one with two scoops of the ice cream. Dust with cocoa powder and serve at once.

Ross Burden
BANANA AND CHOCOLATE MILKSHAKE

This rich drink is more like a dessert. It is likely to be a hit with children and adults alike, so be prepared to make double the quantity.

Serves 2

75 g (3 oz) milk chocolate, broken into squares
2 tbsp double cream
knob butter
2 ripe bananas
2 scoops vanilla ice cream
300 ml (½ pint) milk, well chilled

Melt the chocolate with the cream and butter in the microwave on high for 2 minutes or over a pan of simmering water for 3 minutes. As soon as the mixture has melted, use a spatula to transfer into a fresh, cold bowl and sit it in a dish of ice to cool it down.

Once the chocolate mixture is cool, place it in a liquidizer. Peel and slice the bananas, then add to the liquidizer with the ice cream and milk. Blend until smooth, then pour into tall tumbler glasses. Serve with a straw.

James Tanner
ORANGE DAIQUIRI

This cocktail is very easy to make. It is a refreshing thirst-quencher and goes down well at a drinks party. It could be made with a can of pineapple chunks in natural juice instead of the oranges. ▶

Serves 2

4 oranges
3 tbsp double cream
1 miniature bottle light rum (about 50 ml (2 fl oz) in total)
good handful ice cubes

Cut the peel and all the white pith from two of the oranges and then cut the flesh into segments. Place in a liquidizer and squeeze in the juice from the two remaining oranges.

Add the cream, rum and ice cubes to the liquidizer and blend until the ice is crushed. Pour into tall cocktail glasses to serve.

Paul Rankin
WHITE WINE SPRITZER

This is a refreshing twist on an old favourite. You could use a mixture of orange and lemon, but I prefer the sharpness of the lemon.

Serves 2

1 lemon
4 fresh basil leaves
2 tbsp caster sugar
6 ice cubes
200 ml (7 fl oz) dry white wine
200 ml (7 fl oz) soda or sparking water

Cut the lemon into small pieces, discarding any pips, and place in a mini food processor or liquidizer with the basil, sugar and ice cubes. Blend to a pulp.

Divide the lemon pulp between tall glasses and pour in the white wine. Top up with soda or sparkling water and stir to combine. Serve at once.

Brian Turner
BAILEYS AND BANANA DREAMBOAT

Baileys Irish Cream is a unique blend of cream and whiskey with a touch of chocolate and vanilla.

Serves 2

50 g (2 oz) plain chocolate
2 ripe miniature bananas
100 ml (3½ fl oz) Baileys Irish Cream
2 tbsp maple syrup
100 g (4 oz) Greek yoghurt
100 ml (3½ fl oz) milk
good handful ice cubes

Break the chocolate into squares and melt it in a heatproof bowl set over a pan of simmering water for 3 minutes or on high in the microwave for 2 minutes. Leave to cool a little and then swirl around two tall glasses and set aside for 5 minutes to set.

Peel and slice the bananas and add to a liquidizer. Add the Baileys, maple syrup, yoghurt, milk and ice and blend until smooth. Pour the dreamboat into the chocolate-decorated glasses and serve.

James Martin
COSMOPOLITAN COCKTAIL

A potent party drink.

Serves 2

100 g (4 oz) cranberries, thawed if frozen
1 miniature bottle Grand Marnier (about 50 ml (2 fl oz) in total)
good handful ice cubes
finely grated rind and juice 2 limes
4 tbsp caster sugar

Put two Martini glasses in the freezer. Place the cranberries in a liquidizer with the Grand Marnier, ice cubes, and half the lime juice and sugar. Blend until smooth. Pass through a fine sieve into a jug, pressing with the back of a wooden spoon to get all the juice.

Place the remaining lime juice in one saucer, and mix the lime rind with the remaining sugar in another. Take the glasses from the freezer and dip the tops in the lime juice, then in the lime-flavoured sugar. Pour the Cosmopolitans into the frosted glasses to serve.

Brian Turner
LIME AND MINT VODKA

This is a refreshing drink, but beware – although it goes down easily it is very alcoholic. ◄

Serves 2

small bunch fresh mint, plus extra sprigs to decorate
1 lime, cut into slices
2 tbsp caster sugar
1 miniature bottle vodka (about 50 ml (2 fl oz) in total)
about 150 g (5 oz) ice cubes
600 ml (1 pint) soda water

Strip the mint leaves into a cocktail shaker or tall, sturdy jug. Add the lime slices and sugar, then, using the end of a rolling pin, muddle together to form a lumpy pulp. Pour in the vodka and fill up with ice, then shake or stir until very well chilled.

Half-fill tall glasses with fresh ice cubes and strain over the chilled lime vodka, then top up with soda water. Decorate with mint sprigs to serve.

Phil Vickery
BUCK'S FIZZ

Named after London's Buck's Club, where it was first served in 1921, this is the English version of the French Mimosa. It is usually served at brunch but seems to go down well at any time.

Serves 2

2 oranges
splash grenadine
about 200 ml (7 fl oz) Champagne or cava (ice cold)

Cut the oranges in half and squeeze out the juice into a bowl, then pass through a fine strainer into a jug. Divide between two Champagne glasses and add a dash of grenadine to each one.

Top up with the Champagne or cava and serve at once.

Ross Burden
COINTREAU AND MANDARIN SMOOTHIE

The mandarins give this cocktail body. It's refreshing but don't get too carried away – it is easy to drink, but deceptively strong.

Serves 2

400 g (14 oz) can mandarins in light syrup
1 miniature bottle Cointreau (50ml (2 fl oz) in total)
50 ml (2 fl oz) double cream, well chilled
2 tbsp mascarpone cheese
handful ice cubes
about 6 cranberries
icing sugar, to dust

Place the mandarins and their syrup in a liquidizer with the Cointreau, double cream, mascarpone and ice. Blend to a frothy purée, then pour into tall glasses to serve.

Lightly crush the cranberries and decorate each glass with them. Dust with icing sugar to create a 'snowy' effect and serve immediately.

Gino D'Acampo
MULLED WINE

For any winter celebration – this is a great way to warm people as they come in from the cold.

Serves 2–4

4 oranges
600 ml (1 pint) red wine
2 tbsp caster sugar
1 cinnamon stick
6 whole cloves
1 lemon

Cut three of the oranges in half and squeeze out the juice. Place in a pan with the red wine and sugar.

Break the cinnamon stick in half and add to the pan with the cloves. Heat gently for about 5 minutes to allow the flavours to combine, stirring occasionally until the sugar has dissolved.

Meanwhile, cut the remaining orange and the lemon in half and then cut into slices. Ladle the mulled wine into heatproof glasses and add a couple of orange and lemon slices to each one to serve.

Lesley Waters
BOOZY COFFEE TODDY

This is a special treat. For me there's nothing nicer after a hard day's work. ▶

Serves 2

1 sachet freshly ground coffee (for a 2-cup cafetière)	Make enough coffee to fill a small cafetière (2-cup size). Place the cream in a bowl and lightly whip.
50 ml (2 fl oz) double cream, well chilled	
1 miniature bottle white rum (about 50 ml (2 fl oz) in total)	Pour two tablespoons of the rum into each coffee cup, add a teaspoon of muscovado sugar to each, top up with hot coffee and stir.
2 tsp light muscovado sugar	Carefully pour a layer of cream onto each cup, over the back of a spoon, and sprinkle with the grated chocolate. Serve immediately with a square or two of chocolate on the side.
25 g (1 oz) plain chocolate, grated, plus extra to serve	

Ross Burden
PIÑA COLADA

A *Ready Steady Cook* version of a truly decadent cocktail.

Serves 2

1 miniature pineapple	Cut off the leaf crown and bottom of the pineapple so that it sits flat. Using a sharp knife, remove the skin by cutting down the length of the fruit. Cut the flesh into slices and remove the woody core. Reserve two slices for decoration and dice the remainder, then place in a liquidizer. Add the Malibu to the liquidizer with the coconut ice cream and blitz until smooth.
1 miniature bottle Malibu (about 50 ml (2 fl oz) in total)	
2 scoops coconut ice cream	
2 natural glacé cherries, to decorate	

Pour into large-bowled glasses and decorate with a slice of pineapple and a glacé cherry before serving immediately.

Antony Worrall Thompson
CHOCOLATE EGGNOG WITH BRANDY

Eggnog is a classic Christmas tipple that seems to be made at least once in our house every festive season. I was lucky enough to get a bar of Valrhona dark chocolate in the quickie bag, which made this all the more special.

Serves 2

400 ml (14 fl oz) milk	Place the milk, cream, eggs and sugar in a small heavy-based pan and heat gently for 6–8 minutes or until the mixture is thick enough to coat the back of a wooden spoon.
400 ml (14 fl oz) double cream	
2 eggs	
50 g (2 oz) caster sugar	Meanwhile, melt the chocolate in a non-metallic bowl in the microwave on high for 2 minutes or set over a pan of simmering water for 3 minutes.
75 g (3 oz) plain chocolate, broken into squares	
1 miniature bottle brandy (about 50 ml (2 fl oz) in total)	Drizzle the melted chocolate around the inside of each tall glass and leave for a minute or two to set. Pour the brandy into the bottom of the glasses and top up with the eggnog to serve.

'Feeling brandy?'

the ten-minute cookbook

INDEX

the ten-minute cookbook